The Larger Bulbs

Brian Mathew

THE LARGER BULBS

B. T. Batsford   London
Published in association with
The Royal Horticultural Society

This is for
Maggie and Paul
as a small compensation for all the
hours I spend with my head in a bulb frame

First published 1978
© Brian Mathew, 1978

ISBN 0 7134 1246 1

Printed and bound by Cox & Wyman Limited, Fakenham
for the publishers
B. T. Batsford Ltd, 4 Fitzhardinge Street,
London W1H 0AH

Foreword

By C. D. Brickell, Director, The Royal Horticultural Society's Garden, Wisley

In his new work Brian Mathew complements and expands upon the wide range of bulbous species described in his earlier book, *Dwarf Bulbs.* He provides here a stimulating and informative account of the larger bulbs, which cannot fail to help the many gardeners already growing some members of this fascinating group of plants, as well as those whose interest has yet to be awakened.

In a work which encompasses such a wide spectrum of the world's flora, the selection must necessarily be limited, and Brian Mathew has wisely confined himself fairly strictly to those species and their variants which he knows from personal experience and has grown himself.

Wisely, too, he has not attempted to involve his readers in the morass of hybrids and cultivars which abound in widely cultivated genera such as *Lilium*, *Narcissus* and *Tulipa*, a task far beyond the limits the author has set for this book. This does not mean that *The Larger Bulbs* will be unrewarding to specialists in these groups; far from it, as the accounts of the species included are botanically authoritative and include most useful cultivation details of interest to all growers of bulbous plants. Particularly valuable to the bulb enthusiast will be the information on unusual genera like *Gelasine* and *Mastigostyla* which is not to my knowledge readily available elsewhere to gardeners.

Although many of the bulbous plants described are hardy outside in British gardens, it is pleasing to find mention of a good selection of those requiring cool greenhouse or conservatory treatment which were at one time widely grown but are now seldom seen. A number like *Gloriosa*, *Hymenocallis* and *Stenomesson* are easily grown as pot-plants, requiring only mild heat to thrive, and it is to be hoped that the many gardeners who have conservatories or greenhouses will be encouraged to try them as a result of reading this stimulating book.

Contents

The Illustrations

Colour illustrations are marked by an asterisk
(Black and white illustrations are between pages 96 and 97. The colour plates
face pages 64 and 65, 80 and 81)

Tigridia bicolor
Tigridia galanthoides
Tigridia vanhouttei
* Trillium sessile
Triteleia ixioides
* Veltheimia bracteata
* Veltheimia bracteata 'Rosalba'

Line illustrations

Acknowledgments

To record here all those who have helped in the preparation of this book would be impossible, for I would have to pay tribute to every past and present collector, botanist or gardener who has searched for, described or cultivated bulbous plants. Without the painstaking efforts of these people there would be no herbarium specimens for us to refer to, no names or descriptions to facilitate identification and no cultivation hints from the pages of the past.

For this reason I have decided to mention only those from whom I have obtained living material, and even so the list is considerable and almost certainly incomplete. I apologize to anyone who is left out, but they can be assured that I am grateful for every item I have been given.

For Mediterranean, Near and Middle East collections the names of Paul and Polly Furse, Professor T. Hewer, Professors T. and A. Baytop, Dr P. H. Davis, Chris Grey-Wilson, Jim Archibald, Oleg Polunin, John Watson, P. M. Synge, Dr J. R. Marr, Dr Martyn Rix and R. D. Nutt come immediately to mind, for their initials and collection numbers occur repeatedly on labels in my bulb frames. Smaller and more specific, but no less important, living collections have been made by Erich Pasche and Dr H. Leep in Turkey, Martin Young in the Cyclades, John Ingham in Iran, Vic Horton in the Iberian and Balkan peninsulars and Herbert and Molly Crook in various corners of Europe. In South Africa, Professor G. Delpierre, Dr Ted Oliver, Mr J. Loubser and Dr M. P. de Vos have helped me to obtain some of the vast number of beautiful bulbous plants, as has Dr Maurice Boussard in France from his extensive collection of Cape *Iridaceae*. Wayne Roderick, Marshall Olbrich, Lester Hawkins, Dr R. W. Cruden, Sally Walker, Caryn Ecker, David Hunt, Fred Boutin, Roy Davidson, Marcia Wilson, James Bauml and Dr T. Howard have sent me many of the beautiful Californian and Mexican species; while farther south in the Americas, the gatherings of Dr Otto Zöllner, Dr P. F. Ravenna, John Watson, Pamela Holt, S. G. Saunders, Dr B. K. Blount and Ralph Palmer have enriched the range of New World bulbs now in cultivation here in Britain. Don Elick and Seiko Takuma in Japan have sent some of the rarely seen species from that botanically fascinating country. Most of the Russian species I have obtained have originated from the seed lists of the various State botanic gardens and I am grateful to their directors for making these available. For Russian plants I must in particular thank Dr E. Gabrielian of Yerevan, Dr H. Mordak of Leningrad and Miss L. Asiechvili of Tbilisi for their co-operation, and Milan

Prasil of Czechoslovakia for his collection from the Caucasus. Ken and Lesley Gillanders have helped by sending some of the Australian species.

For various treasured items from their own private collections of bulbs I thank Chris Lovell, Paul Christian, Michael Hoog, late of van Tubergen Ltd, and those two greatly missed plantsmen Eliot Hodgkin and E. B. Anderson to whom I owe much of my early enthusiasm for bulbs.

A lot of valuable information has been gained by 'bulbous chat' with my friends and colleagues Wessel Marais, Chris Brickell and Desmond Meikle who have also generously shared with me plants from their own collections.

I am grateful to the Director and to the Keeper of the Herbarium, Royal Botanic Gardens, Kew, for the use of the unrivalled herbarium collections and paintings of petaloid monocotyledons which have been of the utmost help.

The line drawings have been prepared by Pat Halliday and I am grateful to her for happily agreeing to illustrate some of the more ungainly species such as the 'drumstick' *Allium* species.

My greatest thanks go to Maggie for translating my chaotic manuscript into typescript and for tolerating my oft-repeated mutter, 'I ought to be writing!'

The author and publishers would like to thank the following for permission to reproduce black and white photographs: T. Walker (*Milla biflora*) and M. Young (*Pancratium maritimum*); and for colour photographs, Ernest Crowson (*Trillium sessile*); Valerie Finnis (*Pancratium illyricum*); T. F. Hewer (*Allium rosenbachianum*); M. Hoog (*Veltheimia bracteata* and *Veltheimia bracteata* 'Rosalba'); W. J. Lewis Palmer (*Dierama pendula*); Harry Smith (*Arisaema cordidissimum, Camassia esculenta* and *Nerine bowdeni*); and the Royal Horticultural Society in whose *Journal* many of the colour photographs originally appeared. The remaining photographs are from the author's own collection.

Preface

If, as I said in the preface to *Dwarf Bulbs*, the term was as nebulous a title as one could choose for a book, then *The Larger Bulbs* must surely approach the ridiculous! However, short of a mighty series of tomes covering all bulbous plants, I can see no other way of introducing an enthusiast's bulb book dealing with those species which are anything but dwarf. To attempt to place height limits in centimetres on the plants to be included would be hopeless for, as anyone who knows anything about bulbous plants will agree, their dimensions can vary enormously within one species depending on conditions of growth. As in *Dwarf Bulbs*, I have taken the term 'bulb' not in the strict botanical sense but in the parlance of horticulturists and nurserymen, so that you may find corms, tubers, rhizomes and swollen storage roots together with true bulbs in the following pages.

I feel no need to apologize for this approach, for I know that I would be open to even more ridicule if the book was one of a series entitled *Larger Corms, Larger Rhizomes*, etc. My main aim is, after all, only to provide an informative but chatty, readable book about this popular group of monocotyledonous plants, not a learned revision of each and every genus involved – a task which will surely not be completed by anyone in my lifetime! Neither did I set out with the intention of producing a checklist of all the species in each genus, and even less so their hybrids, since in the ever-changing world of horticulture cultivars come and go fairly rapidly and an up-to-date nurseryman's catalogue can provide most of the answers in that respect. With a few genera such as *Narcissus, Lilium* and *Gladiolus*, it is best for the enthusiast to become involved in a specialist society to keep up with the latest advancements in hybridization.

It is surprising how many of the taller species of bulbs are not hardy in the cooler temperate regions, but presumably this is because the warmer regions where the plants occur wild are favourable for more robust growth, whereas the dwarf species are the result of harsher conditions of cold or drought. Thus it is very noticeable that many tall *Lilium* species are either woodland plants or occur in warm temperate or subtropical zones which receive some summer rain, while most of the tiny *Crocus* species occur wild in exposed, rather cold or dry places and obtain most of their moisture in winter and spring. Of course, there are exceptions – it would be a fool who believed that he could lay down rules in the totally variable world of plants!

The taller bulbs also, quite understandably, take longer on average to grow each season up to the flowering stage than dwarf species do, so they tend to flower rather later in the season. Most Lilies are therefore summer flowering although they start to grow in spring, while most dwarf bulbs such as *Iris*, *Crocus* and *Galanthus* all grow rapidly and flower in early spring after the cold winters and before the onset of warm dry summers. The book contains quite a lot of plants which cannot be grown without the aid of a heated greenhouse, but it is worth experimenting if you have a warm border at the foot of a south wall or fence. Those species which are dormant through the winter are, of course, much the easier to deal with since the problem of frost damage to foliage or developing inflorescence does not arise. For this reason I have included quite a number of South African species from the Eastern Cape which are 'summer growers' and therefore suitable for outdoor cultivation here.

Orchids are omitted, partly because they are such a specialized topic and really require a book of their own, and partly because there are very few tall hardy ones anyway.

As with *Dwarf Bulbs*, I have omitted the authorities for the names – that is, the names of the botanists who first described the species in question. The book is not an attempt at extreme botanical precision and it is in only a few cases where confusion may arise that it is felt necessary to include the authority after the specific name.

I have followed botanical revisions where they are available but otherwise have dealt with the species under their most generally accepted names. Many genera are still in need of taxonomic review but this is not the place to attempt such a formidable task and with most bulbous plants it is essential to study wild populations in order to obtain a clear view of the variability within each species. Herbarium specimens of this group of plants are on the whole very poor as the flowers are of such a flimsy texture. Careful pressing can and does nowadays produce useful material, but it is still essential to know the living plant as well in order to interpret the flattened remains into a three-dimensional shape. Thus where possible I have worked from fresh material for a basic description and then added the range of variation based on the measurements and field notes of herbarium specimens. I have to admit that at times the horticulturist in me finds it hard to accept the multitude of forms which can exist in one species, but the evidence supplied by scores of herbarium specimens is unquestionable and the taxonomist inside usually wins the day!

Introduction

1. Bulbs in Britain

A study of the major centres of distribution of bulbous (in the widest sense) plants in the world reveals that they are confined to areas which experience a period of climatic hardship such as drought or cold, or both. A plant evolves into a species possessing a storage system in order that it can enter a dormant state and remain so until suitable conditions occur for it to commence growth once more. This might be at the onset of a rainy season or when warmer weather begins. Growth is then very rapid so that flowers and seeds can be produced before the next critical period. In high mountain areas which have a dry warm spell following sub-zero temperatures this is important, for in places such as the Turkish Anatolian plateau the period suitable for active growth may be limited to only two months, using water from the melting snows. With many bulbous plants the dormant period is also important for it is then that the buds for the next season are initiated, often inside the bulb or at least in the dormant growing-point. This bud production is in many cases dependent not only on the healthy growth of the leaves in the previous season but on the temperature attained during the rest period. This can be quite critical, especially in the Amaryllidaceae. In extreme cases bulbs will sometimes remain completely dormant with no leaf or flower production if no suitable dormancy treatment is given. I have experienced this with *Narcissus tazetta*, which flowers poorly after a cool damp summer or if it is planted in a position where the soil temperature stays fairly low. Bulb frames, where glass covers keep off excess rain in summer and trap more heat from the sun, provide a useful way of overcoming this problem. Some species I have grown have been extreme in this and have not broken their dormancy until I 'baked' the bulbs on a shelf in the top of the greenhouse for a whole summer. A radiator shelf can also be useful for this purpose, especially for those bulbs which are dormant during our winters.

There are, of course, many exceptions to these general rules and it is necessary to have a knowledge of the native habitat and the climatic conditions which the plant experiences in the wild before the gardener can decide on the method of cultivation. Occasionally, species are found in such extremely damp conditions that it is not very obvious why they have bulbs or other storage organs at all. For example, in Iran I have seen *Gladiolus* in streamside meadows with their corms almost under water, and *Bellevalia pycnantha* grows in similar conditions.

The most ridiculous to my knowledge is *Crinum natans* in which the bulbs grow in stream beds and the long narrow leaves trail, ribbon-like, in the water.

The main areas of distribution of bulbs are the Mediterranean regions, the Middle East and central southern Russia, South Africa, the Pacific States of North America and Mexico, and to a lesser extent South America. A few less important areas occur but only a few genera are involved. For example, *Lilium* has a large number of species in the Himalayas, China and Japan but there are few other bulbous plants in the same area. In tropical Africa most of the bulbs are confined to the eastern countries which have long dry seasons, but even here there are not vast numbers of species considering the large area involved.

One major difficulty which gardeners have when they attempt to grow bulbs which do not occur naturally in their own part of the world is the reversal of seasons. This may involve a change from hemisphere to hemisphere or from one climatic zone to another. Again, a knowledge of the local climate is essential. In South Africa, for example, the south-west Cape species receive winter rainfall and flower mostly between August and October and in Britain they continue to grow through our winter. Thus they are best kept dormant here until about September, then watered until flowering-time which is usually March to June; a change of about six months, which is what one would expect. The species from the eastern Cape receive summer rainfall and in the northern hemisphere they are somewhat easier to grow than the south-west Cape species since they make their growth through our summer months and are dormant during the winter. They can therefore be lifted and kept dry in a frost-free shed or left out throughout the year in mild districts, since the resting bulbs are below ground away from the frost in the worst weather.

Most Mediterranean and Middle East bulbs experience winter rains, as do those from western America. Consequently they require similar conditions to the south-west Cape species, although they are mostly much hardier and can be grown out of doors or in an unheated bulb frame or alpine house.

Many of the larger Mexican and South American bulbs behave as summer-growers in Britain, and can therefore be grown out of doors and lifted for the winter. *Tigridia* and *Cypella*, for example, are very satisfactory when treated in this way, although they are better left undisturbed in a mild place, or planted out in a cool greenhouse border.

2. Cultivation Methods

The following section should be regarded as a general guide to the methods which can be tried for the cultivation of bulbs rather than explicit instructions for the treatment of individual species. Obviously my experience is limited to the areas I have lived or worked in and my recommendations may well have little bearing on what happens in a garden in North America, or even in another part of southern England. The microclimate of a particular garden is often more important than the overall weather pattern of a large area and it is best for the would-be cultivator of a particular species to first obtain a knowledge of the wild habitat of that plant. After all, the species has almost certainly evolved to suit a particular environment so it is up to us to fool it into believing that it is still there! Please, therefore, regard the following as tentative suggestions as to the various ways in which bulbs might be utilized and experiment with various species in various situations.

Lastly, one general word about the planting depth of bulbs. They can on the whole be planted fairly deeply, this having the dual advantage of keeping them away from the frosty surface of the soil and delaying emergence of the young shoots as long as possible. It is not unusual, for example, to find tulip bulbs, in the wild, at a depth of 25–30 centimetres, and although this is perhaps exceptional most bulbs grow at least 8–10 centimetres deep.

BULBS IN GRASS

Undoubtedly one of the most attractive ways of growing the more hardy and tolerant species is to naturalize them in grass. Many species will grow satisfactorily in this way, and if one has an area which can be left as rough grass it is well worth experimenting with any surplus bulbs. The main drawback is, of course, that the grass cannot be mown until the bulbs have finished their growth, and with larger bulbs which are usually later flowering than dwarf species it may mean that the area must be left for most of the summer. A scattering of bonemeal in early spring is a good idea as this will feed the bulbs during their growing season. Unfortunately it does not discriminate and the grass will also become more robust as a result. Larger bulbs which I have seen growing well in grass are: *Narcissus* spp., *Allium dioscoridis*, *Camassia* species, *Fritillaria* species (the more robust ones such as *F. pyrenaica*), *Ornithogalum pyrenaicum*, *O. narbonense*, *Lilium szovitsianum*, *L. pyrenaicum*, *L. martagon* and its varieties, *Leucojum aestivum*, *Tulipa sprengeri*, *T. sylvestris*, *Gladiolus byzantinus*. I imagine that many more would be satisfactory since this is the natural way for many of them to grow. For bulbs which prefer dryish conditions in summer while they are dormant this method of cultivation is helpful, for the grass uses up any excess moisture in the soil in damp weather. In winter the turf provides added protection from frost, which bare soil does not give.

A simple planting method is to mark out strips of turf with a spade, then by sliding the spade under the turf it can be rolled up like a carpet. The soil beneath is loosened with a fork, and if necessary peat or sand incorporated. The bulbs are then planted in the normal manner, so that the top of the bulb is about 4 centimetres below the surface, the soil is firmed down and the turf strip rolled back over. Rolling with a light garden roller, or even a lawn mower with the blade held up off the ground, is sufficient to level the turf again.

It is fun to scatter surplus seed of any bulbous plants in grass, bearing in mind that it might be four or five years before any flower spikes appear.

BORDERS

Any areas where there is little disturbance of the soil is suitable for growing bulbs. This is not because the bulbs necessarily prefer a lack of disturbance but mainly because they are a nuisance! Anyone who has tried to dig between herbaceous plants or shrubs in winter will, I'm sure, agree that there is nothing more annoying than to spike a bulb every time you push in the fork. It is not good for the well-being of the bulbs or the gardener! Groups of bulbs such as lilies can be very effective in between shrubs or herbaceous plants, but mark them well and instead of cultivating the patch, top dress the area with a suitable compost enriched with a granular slow-release fertilizer such as a 'National Growmore' mixture. The compost can be varied depending on the species: for example, lilies prefer a peat or leafmould top-dressing, especially the stem-rooting species (see under *Lilium* for description), while for *Allium* and *Fritillaria* species a well-drained soil and a sandy top-dressing is better. The tender species which grow and flower in summer can be planted out in late spring in gaps between other plants and then lifted again before the autumn frosts. In this case the soil can be prepared during the winter months with compost and fertilizer dug in, so that no top-dressing is necessary. Examples of bulbs treated in this way are *Galtonia*, *Gladiolus* (tender species) including those formerly known as *Acidanthera*, *Hymenocallis*, *Ornithogalum saundersiae* and *Tigridia*.

Any of the plants mentioned above for cultivation in grass are suitable for borders, and many others such as *Allium*, *Arisaema*, *Crinum*, *Crocosmia*, *Curtonus*, *Dracunculus*, *Fritillaria*, *Leucojum*, *Lilium*, *Narcissus*, *Nomocharis*, *Ornithogalum* and *Tulipa*.

The late Mr E. B. Anderson recognized the advantage of planting bulbs among shrubs and trees, where any excess moisture would be taken up by the tree roots. This does not, of course, apply to those bulbs such as *Leucojum aestivum* which prefer damp situations.

SUNNY WALL BEDS

In most 'ordinary' gardens beds situated at the foot of hot sunny walls or fences are fairly restricted in number and size, therefore it is obvious that the owner of such a select spot will want to choose only the best and most suitable species to plant there. If the bed is raised above the level of the surrounding ground so that it is well drained, this is even better, especially if the natural soil is rather heavy. The choice of plants to grow in such a bed is a wide one, so we must really restrict the selection to those which either need a good baking during their dormant summer spell or a little extra shelter in the winter. Larger bulbs which are ideally suited for a sunny sheltered bed include *Fritillaria imperialis* and its varieties, *F. persica*, *F. raddeana*; *Allium regelii*, *A. altissimum* (or any of the showy tall species with large spherical inflorescences); *Tigridia pavonia*;

Rigidella orthantha (in the south of England only); *Amaryllis belladonna*; *Nerine bowdenii*; *Cypella herbertii*; *Lilium pomponium*; *Arisaema candidissimum*; *Tulipa saxatilis*; *Pancratium illyricum*; *Gladiolus natalensis*; *Moraea spathulata*; *Dracunculus*, and the wild forms of *Narcissus tazetta* which are very graceful and beautifully scented but do require a sun-baked position to flower well.

ROCK GARDENS AND BULB FRAMES

In general, the taller species of bulb are not suitable for the average-sized rock garden or bulb frame since they look rather out of proportion and in a frame there is not enough headroom for the plants to develop properly. There may be a case for planting one or two bold groups of something striking in a large rock pocket to stand out among more dwarf alpine plants. Species such as *Tulipa sprengeri*, *Lilium martagon*, *Fritillaria persica*, *Iris magnifica* or *Leucojum aestivum* can be used quite effectively in this way. In a very large alpine garden with rocks of massive proportions, many of the *Narcissus*, *Tulipa* and *Lilium* species would look well when planted in front of a dark rock background.

For species which require a good summer baking, a bulb frame may be necessary for their successful cultivation. A few of the taller Juno *Iris*, for instance, may not be satisfactory in damp areas. Arrangements must be made to provide as much headroom as possible in this case, using 'dutch-barn' shaped frame lights. However, the problem with most bulbs of this type is in providing warm dry summer conditions when the plants are dormant, so the glass lights can be removed completely in the spring when they are making their maximum growth and then replaced after the plant dies back.

Since bulb frames are usually of practical rather than ornamental value, it is wise to plant in rows and to keep a plan for reference, and I find that it is essential to prevent anything from seeding itself or chaos soon results. With most northern hemisphere bulbs the annual treatment of the frames consists of keeping the lights on through the summer months to give the bulbs a good baking, then in early autumn giving the first good watering to encourage new root action. No further watering may then be necessary until early spring. During the winter months the lights are removed whenever the temperature is above freezing and the weather reasonably dry. In spring the frames are left open all the time, unless there is an exceptionally inclement spell, and they can remain off until the foliage begins to yellow and dry off, when they are replaced again for the summer months. An annual feed of bonemeal in autumn before the first watering is all that is necessary, and replanting is only required when the bulbs become too crowded, usually after three or four years.

If a portion of the frame is set aside for summer-flowering bulbs, such as *Tigridia*, *Zephyranthes* and some east Cape species, then a different pattern of treatment is dictated. The lights should be left on during the winter and the soil kept as dry as possible; then they are removed in spring and water is given until the leaves turn yellow in autumn. With tender species it may be necessary to cover the bulbs with bracken or peat fibre in winter.

BULBS IN POTS

Generally speaking, the larger robust growing bulbs are not suitable for pot cultivation; but if one has the space and time it is the safest way of maintaining a collection of rare bulbs as they can be given individual treatment and are easily kept apart, which is not easy to achieve with bulbs planted out in the garden or frames. If pot cultivation is chosen it must be borne in mind that much more attention will be needed in the form of careful watering, repotting every year and feeding during the growing season.

I find it unnecessary to have a wide range of composts to suit individual species and my basic soil mixture is similar to John Innes No 1. Providing it is well-drained, any loam-peat-sand mixture will do, with a slow-release low-nitrogen fertilizer added. I have used some of the proprietary brands of loam-less compost with success but the very peaty ones need some sharp sand or grit added and tend to dry out too much in clay pots so that plastic ones are preferable. On the whole I find that clay pots and a well-drained loam-based compost are the most successful combination. The pots are best plunged in sand or ashes if kept in a cold frame or alpine house where they are likely to be frozen, but with those tender bulbs grown in a heated greenhouse this is unnecessary and the pots are ideally spaced out on a bench to allow a free flow of air around the plants. Unfortunately I have to admit that I do not practise what I preach, and my own greenhouse is invariably solid with pots from end to end!

For heating purposes an electric fan is useful since it also keeps the air moving and, if fitted with a thermostat, can be set to cut in at various temperatures depending upon the cold-tolerance of the bulbs in the house. Larger greenhouses can be sectioned off if necessary so that various temperatures can be maintained for different species. Most bulbs have a dormant period, or at least a dryish spell even if they do not actually die right down (e.g. *Veltheimia bracteata*, *Vallota speciosa*), and a knowledge of the natural environmental conditions helps when deciding on the watering/drying-out regime to be adopted.

Re-potting of bulbs is almost always carried out at the end of the dormant season, just before the plants come into growth again. It is not advisable to re-pot at the start of the rest period, for the bulb then has to remain in new loose dry soil for several months and may in consequence shrivel badly. The depth at which bulbs are potted is not very critical but they should certainly have a good covering of at least 1 centimetre and the robust species should be about 5–10 centimetres deep, especially if they are stem-rooting lilies.

The larger species can be most attractive when grown in big pots or wooden tubs for standing out on a patio or in a conservatory. Some of the lilies are very suitable for this purpose, as are *Gloriosa* and *Sandersonia*. Unless they contain very hardy species, the tubs should be stored away in a frost-free place for the winter. Re-potting is not essential every year but a top-dressing of slow-release fertilizer is necessary if healthy growth is to be maintained.

3. *Propagation*

It is important that the owner of a collection of bulbs makes some attempt to increase them, either with a view to selling some or passing some on to friends in order to spread them around in cultivation, or to give him enough to experiment with varying methods of cultivation.

SEEDS

Many bulbous plants do not increase vegetatively and the only way to increase them is by seed. It is best to pollinate all the less common species by hand since one cannot rely on local insects pollinating a non-native species. Even if the seeds are not required for home use there are always plenty of takers for the excess, and the Alpine Garden Society is keen to receive any surplus seeds for its excellent annual seed list, which is also a good source of rare species. Personally I prefer to try to increase the species rather than attempting cross-pollination with a view to producing hybrids. In general I believe that wild plants have a grace and sense of proportion which is often lost in their un-natural hybrids, although of course in some cases very fine garden plants have been raised which are easier to grow than their wild ancestors. If any crossing is undertaken, it is important to keep records so that the origin of any new hybrids is known.

Having obtained seeds, whether gathered fresh or obtained at a later date from someone else, it is best to sow them straight away, for if they are kept for a few months germination may be delayed for an extra year. My method of sowing is the same for all bulbs, and very simple. Usually the quantity is fairly small and I sow into pots. They must be sown thinly, both to prevent damping-off in the seedling stage through overcrowding and to ensure that the bulbs are spaced out reasonably when they increase in size. After some experience I have now come to the conclusion that once germination has taken place and the seedlings have rooted well it is best to knock out the pot full of young bulbs and plant them out in the open ground, bulb frame or greenhouse border where they are to grow on. Thus they should be well-spaced at sowing time. Any species which is to stay in pots for its entire life can be treated in the same way, the whole pot of seedlings being knocked out and potted on with as little disturbance as possible.

Having chosen a suitable size of pot, place a crock over the hole and fill to within about 1 centimetre of the rim with a free-draining compost such as John

Innes which has a little extra sharp sand added. The seeds are then sown and covered with grit which should be about 3 millimetres in diameter, this giving an ideal medium for the young shoots to push through. With this covering there is never any difficulty with the soil surface becoming compacted, moss and liverwort are discouraged, and weed seeds falling on to the grit surface are less likely to germinate. The subsequent treatment of the pots depends upon the species. Most of those which originate in cold-winter countries require frosty conditions to trigger off the germination process. With these I prefer to plunge the pots out of doors until germination has occurred, then move them into a frame or greenhouse until the weather improves and the seedlings can be planted out. With tender species a period of frost is, of course, unnecessary and these are kept in the greenhouse right from the time of sowing, although they can be planted out in summer.

As indicated above, I prefer to plant out the complete pot of seedlings during the first growing season after germination. If, however, they are kept in pots for more than one year, they must have some extra nourishment in the second season. I scatter some granules of a slow-release, low-nitrogen fertilizer on the surface of the pots at the end of the dormant season and the plant foods are then washed down during the subsequent waterings. Another point to remember if the young bulbs are left in pots is that they tend to keep growing longer than mature bulbs in their first year and therefore need encouraging, since a larger bulb will result at the end of that season. In short, watering should be carefully controlled and the young bulbs not dried out too early. Additionally, be careful not to over-bake these small bulbs for they will not withstand such hot dry conditions in a pot as will a mature bulb which is being baked to encourage it to flower.

The time taken to reach flowering-size from seed varies widely from species to species but it is normally three to five years. Some plants flower very rapidly, *Tigridia pavonia* and *Lilium formosanum* being good examples, for they can be flowered the same season as the seed is sown. At the other extreme, *Tulipa* species can take up to seven years.

NATURAL BULB INCREASE

Some bulbs increase vegetatively satisfactorily and all the offspring will be identical with the parent, whereas with seeds variation might occur. There are three main ways in which new bulbs may be formed vegetatively. The parent bulb may split into two or more new bulbs which are fairly large and take only a short while to grow on to flowering size. Alternatively, the parent may remain and produce several small bulblets around its base. The third way is the production of aerial bulblets on the stem in the axils of the leaves. Any small bulblets, whether aerial or subterranean, can be treated in the same way. They can either be left to grow on *in situ* to form a clump around the original bulb, or they can be detached and grown separately. With the very easily cultivated species, they can be planted straight into their permanent positions, but if they are at all tricky they are best grown on in pots, a bulb frame or greenhouse.

If a particularly interesting form of a species arises and it is considered that seedlings will vary, it might be a good idea to try to encourage bulblet production artificially, unless of course this happens naturally anyway. There are various ways of achieving this and it is worth experimenting if you have more than one bulb. *Lilium* species can be increased from scales quite easily, these being detached from the parent bulb and put into a polythene bag with a small amount of slightly damp peat and kept in a warm shady spot until the young bulbs have formed along the broken surfaces. These can then be detached and grown on in soil in the usual way. Some of the true bulbs, such as *Scilla*, can be encouraged to form young bulblets if the basal plate is cut and pieces of crock inserted to keep the cuts from growing over again. The bulblets appear around the cut scales and the old bulb can be broken up to reveal the new small bulbs, which are then separated and planted up. With *Fritillaria* I have had great success in breaking up the bulbs into separate scales, usually two per bulb. These are planted or potted in well-drained compost and they form reasonably sized bulbs the same season – one can thus double a stock each year in this way.

4. Pests and Diseases

There is no substitute for good cultivation and it must be remembered that bulbs in poor health because of the cultural methods will be very susceptible to attack from various organisms. Some troubles are unavoidable, such as attacks by aphids and slugs, but these are easily cured. Aphids should be controlled rigorously since they carry viruses, and in *Lilium* in particular this is a very serious problem. The modern systemic insecticides are very effective and if a collection of Lily species is being grown it is best to spray as a matter of routine. Diseases of the bulbs are not such a problem nowadays since I find that the systemic fungicide 'Benlate' is an excellent treatment, the bulbs being treated during the dormant period.

Rather than attempting to describe all pests and diseases which can attack bulbs, and recommend treatments which will be out of date in a couple of years, I would rather refer the reader to other publications which deal with the subject in more accurate detail. The Ministry of Agriculture publishes a Bulletin called *Diseases of Bulbs*, No 117, by W. C. Moore. The RHS *Dictionary of Gardening* gives a lot of information, and for Fellows of the RHS there is an advisory service at Wisley. *Horticultural Pests* by Fox Wilson, revised by Dr P. Becker, is an excellent all-round book, not dealing specifically with bulbous plants.

5. *Collecting Bulbs in the Wild*

My first word of advice here is don't, unless you really have to. Obviously it is necessary for botanists to study specimens of known wild origin, and it is also desirable for horticultural purposes to introduce plants which are not already in cultivation. But to go on collecting the same species once they are well-established in cultivation is wrong and pointless, unless for some reason it becomes desirable to bring in a new stock of wild material – perhaps the garden stocks may have become virus-ridden, or have hybridized with related species; in some instances all the plants in cultivation may be clonal, derived vegetatively from one individual, resulting in sterility. Here there is a case for bringing in new wild-source material to encourage seed production in order to give the species 'variation potential' again. This is important, for when we raise plants from seed we are not merely increasing the number, but are introducing the possibility for the species to vary and adapt to its new conditions in cultivation. Those seedlings most suited to their changed environment will survive best and we are assisting them to evolve in this way. One hears the remark about a long-established clonal plant that it is 'losing its vigour through over-propagation': this may be imaginary, and merely a result of forgotten methods of cultivation, or there may be some truth in it, for in selecting one original plant of a clone we at a stroke reduce the gene bank for that particular species and take away its chance to vary and adapt to our ever-changing climate and atmosphere.

Well-regulated collecting can do no harm at all but it is essential that only a small number of plants from each locality is removed. In the past, and perhaps it is still happening, over-enthusiastic collecting has decimated certain species and it is hoped that nowadays with the pressures on wild plants greater than ever before, plant collectors will use restraint. Only as a last resort should the argument that a plant is being preserved in cultivation be necessary – its chosen wild habitat is obviously the correct place for it and every effort should be made to preserve it there. In many instances road-widening and building are largely to blame for the decimation of plants and in such cases there is every reason to collect the plants before this happens.

When advising people on how to collect I do, therefore, add a plea that they should be sparing in their enthusiasm, and only bring back plants if they are sure that they can give them a fair chance of survival. If seed can be collected this affords a very ready method of introducing plants and it takes only one capsule of, for example, a *Lilium* or *Fritillaria* to produce a lot of bulbs in cultivation. The worst time to collect most bulbs is when they are in flower and if it is possible to mark them and return later for a few ripened bulbs and seeds success is far more certain. In this case the treatment is very simply a case of digging up the bulbs and placing them in paper envelopes to dry off. If, however, it is necessary to dig them up whilst in flower – for example to gather particular colour forms – the best method I have found is to keep them damp until they can be potted and then allow them to go dormant in their own time. Polythene bags allow bulbous plants to be kept for a fortnight or more if the roots are kept just moist and the leaves allowed to protrude from the top of the bag. If, during a longer trip, there is no possibility of potting the bulbs, one can induce them into premature dormancy by removing them from the bags for a short while each day to dry them out over a period of a week or two. Alternatively, if it is convenient, a well-marked nursery bed can be made in a shady spot and the bulbs planted there until later in the season. The main thing is to remember exactly where they are, as dormant bulbs can be very difficult to locate if other vegetation has grown up in the meantime.

It is important to keep good field notes, especially if some of the plants are to be used for botanical purposes; the botanist will need to know in particular the exact location and any other relevant information about the habitat such as altitude, soil type, plant associations and so on.

Having achieved the aim of getting the bulbs to the dormant state, the subsequent treatment is essentially the same as that recommended in the chapter on cultivation.

Finally, do not forget that there might be local laws applying to the removal of plants from the wild and that it is necessary to possess a plant importation licence to bring them into Britain.

Alphabetical List

Acidanthera Iridaceae

This genus is not now considered to be distinct from *Gladiolus* and species such as *A. bicolor* and *A. laxiflora* can be found in this book under their correct names, *G. callianthus* and *G. ukambanensis* respectively. The tropical African species of Acidanthera were discussed, and a key provided to their identification, by W. Marais in *Kew Bulletin* 28, 2:311 (1973) in which he recognizes nine species belonging to this group. Only the two species mentioned above are in general cultivation and *G. ukambanensis* is rather rare.

Albuca Liliaceae

Tropical African and South African bulbs of no great horticultural value since they are not hardy in Britain and mostly rather dull. A few, however, may be rather useful in the greenhouse or planted outside in warmer climates. The leaves are all basal and the naked stem has a raceme of flowers, sometimes with very short pedicels so that they form a more spike-like inflorescence. Each flower consists of six segments, the inner three of which, although not joined, lie close together and form a tube which closes over the style and stamens. The outer segments usually diverge more. The usual flower colour is white or greeny-yellow, often with a darker green stripe along the centre of each segment.

A. aurea This grows to between 30 and 60cm in height with linear leaves up to 50cm long and 1–2·5cm wide. The flowers are 2–3cm long, yellow with a broad green stripe on the segments, and are carried on very long pedicels, 6–7cm usually. It occurs wild in the Cape Province in low bush country below 1000m. In Britain it flowers between January and March.

A. canadensis (*A. minor*) In spite of the unfortunately misleading name, this is a South African plant! It grows 20–40cm in height with very greyish leaves about 15cm in length with a broad sheathing base narrowing abruptly to about 1–3cm wide, then tapering gradually to a point. The very lax raceme has up to seven pendulous flowers on long pedicels, each flower 1·5–2cm long, greenish yellow with a green band on each segment. Wild in the south-west Cape below 300m in sandy places. It flowers in March to May in Britain. Although Linnaeus, who first described the species, was apparently aware that the place of origin was in Africa he went ahead and called it 'canadensis', following J. Cornuto who had previously listed it in a book of Canadian plants.

A. major This robust species grows up to 90cm in height with narrow, 1cm wide leaves half as long as the raceme. The raceme is lax with up to twelve 2cm long flowers on pedicels about 4cm in length. Each flower is very substantial with broad segments which are yellow with a green or brownish stripe and the bracts usually also have a reddish tinge. It occurs wild in the south-west Cape in shrubby foothills below 3000m. In Britain it flowers in late winter or early spring.

A. nelsonii This is by far the most massive and striking of the taller species, reaching 150cm with dark, slightly glaucous, green leaves up to 5cm wide. The many-flowered raceme is densely flowered with upright white brown-striped flowers 3–4cm long on pedicels 5–10cm long. A native of Natal and the eastern Cape, growing in grass near the coast, flowering in May or June in Britain. Since this species comes from a summer rainfall region it might be possible to grow this outside in southern England, lifting the dormant bulbs for the winter months as one would with *Gladiolus*, or other eastern Cape bulbs.

Allium Liliaceae

A very easily recognized genus with the umbels of smallish flowers and onion-like odour when crushed. It is a very large genus of about 500 species and contains some of the most important food plants within the monocotyledons, other than the grass family of course. Onion (*A. cepa*), Spring Onion (*A. fistulosum*), Garlic (*A. sativum*), Leek (*A. porrum*), Chives (*A. schoenoprasum*) and Shallots (*A. ascalonicum*) all belong to this genus. There are, however, many very attractive species worth cultivating and they are usually not difficult. It must be realized that others are terrible weeds and only suitable for 'wild gardening', where they can be left to their own devices. It is my experience that most *Allium* species are best excluded from the bulb frame since they can rapidly take over, although this does not occur with those from the Himalayas which require cool, more moist conditions and are best suited to the rock or peat garden. As a general rule, those species from the Mediterranean region and Asia as far as Afghanistan and the Pamirs, and the North American species, require a dry dormant period in summer. Those from non-Mediterranean Europe and eastern Asia are perfectly happy without a dry summer and in fact the latter species grow and flower at that time of year and are dormant in winter, so they must be kept well supplied with water during summer.

Allium causes some controversy amongst botanists as there is no general agreement as to whether they should belong to Liliaceae, Amaryllidaceae or their own family, Alliaceae, together with a few related genera such as Nothoscordum and Tulbaghia. The possession of a superior ovary gives them an affinity with other Liliaceae, the umbel of flowers would suggest Amaryllidaceae and the pundits who favour Alliaceae are using the two features together to make a separate family. All of this is fairly unimportant since the fact remains that *Allium* and its relations are a distinct entity, whether they are treated as a family, subfamily, tribe or whatever – after all, no one can prove anything and it is all purely a matter of opinion!

Most of the *Allium* species are from the northern hemisphere, where they occur in practically every country. A very few go south of the equator, and these are of no consequence horticulturally.

The tall species on the whole present very few problems in cultivation, although some of those from the dry sun-baked hills of the Middle East do need a good well-drained sunny position in gardens. Most of the larger *Alliums* are bulbous, whereas many of the smaller species have rhizomes. In the following list there will therefore be no mention of the rootstock unless it is anything other than a bulb. Most species flower in May or June.

A. albopilosum See *A. christophii.*

A. altissimum Grows 90–150cm in height with a few basal leaves which are rather attractive in the young stages. They are erect, very bright glossy green with a purplish suffusion towards the base and rather broad, tapering at the base and apex. By flowering time they have started to wither and die back at the tips. The very densely-flowered umbels are about 8cm in diameter and have long-pedicelled starry flowers of a bright pinkish-purple with very prominent purple filaments to the stamens. Each flower is about 1·3cm in diameter. Wild in Russian Central Asia, north-east Iran and north-west Afghanistan at 1200–2300m. My own bulbs were grown from seed from one of the Russian botanic gardens and I find it one of the finest of the large-umbel purple species. It reaches the flowering stage in about three years from seed and is not difficult to grow in a sunny spot.

A. atropurpureum 30–70cm in height when in flower, with several narrowly lanceolate leaves which are usually about half the length of the stem. Flowers small and starry with narrow segments, deep red-wine-coloured, produced in a dense hemispherical umbel 5–7cm in diameter, which becomes almost shuttle-cock-shaped in the fruiting stage. Eastern Europe, especially Bulgaria, Romania and Turkey-in-Europe in grassy and lightly wooded places. An easy species and not unattractive with its richly coloured flowers.

A. atroviolaceum Grows up to 100cm in height with a few 0·6cm wide linear leaves on the lower portion of the stem. The umbel is spherical, about 4cm in diameter and very densely flowered so that the pedicels are not visible. The colour is a deep metallic purple and the individual flowers are about 0·7cm long, bell-shaped but rather constricted at the mouth. It is widespread from Europe to Afghanistan and very easy to grow. Like so many of the taller *Alliums*, the leaves are nearly dead by flowering time so that they look rather tatty. It is perhaps best to grow them behind lower growing plants which hide the scruffiest part of the plant.

A. azureum See *A. caeruleum.*

A. bulgaricum See genus *Nectaroscordum.*

1 **Allium altissimum**

2 **Allium neapolitanum**

3 **Allium roseum**

4 **Nectaroscordum (Allium) dioscoridis**

5 **Allium regelii**

6 **Allium atropurpureum**

A. caeruleum (*A. azureum*) 30–60cm in height with a very tight 3–4cm diameter umbel of many small bright blue flowers. It divides up to form clumps of bulbs but is not invasive. Grows in the Pamirs and Tien Shan Mountains. *A. caesium* is very similar. Both require only a sunny, freely draining spot.

A. calocephalum Described by Per Wendelbo as a new species during the last decade and one of the most curious of the recent introductions in *Allium*. Varies in height from 30–70cm with four or five linear basal leaves about 1–4cm wide. The umbel is rather flattish, 4–8cm in diameter and consists of many creamy-white flowers which have extremely long narrow perianth segments in the outer flowers, about 3–3·5cm long and 0·1cm wide, becoming shorter towards the centre of the umbel. The overall appearance is very 'spidery' and the impression is of a large-flowered composite rather than an onion! It occurs only in northern Iraq between 1300 and 3000m. I have grown this species for only two years and am unable to be specific about its requirements, but since Paul Furse has it growing well out of doors in Kent and Dr J. G. Elliott of Ashford grows it in a pot successfully, it would appear to be a fairly easy plant and one which I hope will become more easily obtainable in the future.

A. caspium A fairly short, striking species with a relatively enormous umbel. Up to 35cm in height but usually 20–25cm. The spherical umbel is 10–20cm in diameter containing many small white or pinkish, rather papery-textured flowers with long-exserted stamens. The huge head looks rather loose because the pedicels are unequal, thus spacing out the flowers somewhat. North-east Iran, Afghanistan, Pakistan, Caucasus and Russian Central Asia. It needs a good warm rest period in summer and appears to require bulb-frame cultivation.

A. christophii (*A. albopilosum*) A beautiful species, particularly useful for drying for winter decoration since the perianth segments of the flowers become rather spiny and long-lasting. The umbel is 12–20cm in diameter on a stem 25–50cm high. Each flower is very starry in appearance with narrow segments, about 2–3cm in diameter, of a deep metallic purplish-blue. The basal leaves are strap-shaped and usually rather hairy. Occurs in north-west Iran and Russian Central Asia. This superb species is not difficult to grow and requires only a position where it will be warm and dry during its summer rest period.

A. cowanii See *A. neapolitanum*.

A. dioscoridis See genus *Nectaroscordum*.

A. elatum See *A. giganteum*.

A. flavum A very variable species ranging from 6–30cm in height. The dwarf forms are useful for rock gardens whereas the taller variants are suitable herbaceous border or wild-garden plants. It is worth looking for good forms since many are rather poor in colour. The best I have is a tall one with very grey foliage and stems, good yellow flowers and a sweet scent. The few cylindrical leaves are scattered up the stem. The umbel is rather graceful with yellow flowers on pendulous pedicels, becoming erect in the fruiting stage. Widespread in southern and eastern Europe in dry stony places up to 2500m. A very easy species for sunny positions.

A. giganteum One of the largest and most striking species of the larger onions with stems up to 200cm in height with basal, slightly glaucous, strap-shaped leaves 5–10cm wide. The spherical umbel is dense, 10–15cm in diameter, the individual flowers small and with obtuse segments, lilac-purple. North-east Iran, north-west Afghanistan and adjacent Russia as far as the Pamir-Alai Mountains. A spectacular species for planting in small groups in a sunny border. *A. macleanii* (*A. elatum*) is very similar but has green leaves, not greyish, and the perianth segments are acute. It occurs in eastern Afghanistan, western Pakistan and Russian Tadjikistan.

A. hirtifolium Another of the tall stately species with a spherical umbel of small starry purple flowers. This grows up to 120cm tall and has strap-like basal leaves which are normally pubescent, up to 5cm wide. The umbel is 8–12cm in diameter with many flowers. West and south-west Iran, where it grows up to 3500m altitude on rocky hillsides. I find this one of the easiest of the tall *Alliums* and still grow bulbs which were collected in Iran on the Bowles Scholarship Expedition in 1963. They set plenty of seeds and take about four years to produce flowering plants. We also collected a white form on the same trip and this is useful for planting against a dark background. *A. stipitatum* is very similar and differs only in having a strongly ribbed flower stem and tapered perianth segments, those of *A. hirtifolium* being more parallel-sided. It grows in eastern Afghanistan, Pakistan and Russia in the Pamir and Tien-Shan Mountains.

A. jesdianum See *A. rosenbachianum*.

A. karataviense Although not very tall, this is of such impressive proportions that it must be included here. It is a highly ornamental species for sunny well-drained places. Leaves, usually two per bulb, produced at ground level, broadly elliptical, up to 10cm wide, greyish with a purplish suffusion, especially on the underside. The flower stem is only 15–20cm in height, with a many-flowered umbel up to 20cm in diameter. The flowers are pale pinkish in colour. Occurs wild in Russian Central Asia.

A. macleanii (*A. elatum*) See *A. giganteum*.

A. macranthum An interesting species, 25–40cm in height, which is scarcely bulbous but has thick fleshy storage roots. The leaves are all basal, narrow and channelled. Although the inflorescence carries only seven to 12 flowers on 2–3cm long pedicels, each flower is 1cm long and of a strong purple colour. They are pendulous when fully open. It grows in western China from 3000m to nearly 6000m altitude. It grows well in cultivation if given a cool position and is most attractive.

A. mirum As I noted in *Dwarf Bulbs*, this is an interesting species of recent introduction but probably only suitable for bulb frame cultivation, although it might succeed on a very well-drained soil in a hot sunny position. The leaves are usually two in number, produced at ground level, and are purplish-grey, elliptical in shape, about 4–8cm wide in the middle and 10–25cm long. The pale brownish-purple or whitish flowers are rather bell-shaped, about 1cm across, and are produced in a very dense-flowered spherical umbel 5–9cm in diameter. Grows in Afghanistan in the Hindu Kush in rocky places up to 3000m.

A. murrayanum I have grown this for many years from bulbs given to me by Sir Frederick Stern, but cannot find its true name. It is possibly an exceptionally fine form of *A. acuminatum*, a western American species, with much broader, less pointed, perianth segments than the species normally has. Grows 20–35cm in height with a few narrow leaves near the base of the stems. The umbel is 6–7cm in diameter with flattish bright-pink flowers 1·5–2cm across. A useful and attractive plant for naturalizing around shrubs, although it needs plenty of light to increase and flower well.

A. neapolitanum Rather tender, but will survive all but exceptional winters in the south of England and is a graceful plant for warm sunny borders and is very suitable for cutting. Grows up to 35cm in height with a few linear lanceolate basal leaves and a loose 5–7cm diameter umbel of pure white flowers, each 1·5–2cm across. *A. subhirsutum* is smaller in all its parts and although a delicate species it has not the garden value of its more robust relative. *A. cowanii* is a particularly fine form of *A. neapolitanum*, often sold by bulb nurseries.

A. nigrum Grows to 50–100cm in height with a sturdy leafless stem, the basal lanceolate leaves being usually two in number and up to 5cm wide. The umbel is 6–9cm in diameter and hemispherical with many substantial flowers 1–1·5cm across. They are usually pale pinkish-purple but do vary somewhat in depth of colour from near-white. It is widespread in the whole Mediterranean region, often in fields. *A. orientale* is like a smaller white-flowered version of this, with a stem rarely exceeding 35cm and an inflorescence up to 5cm in diameter. There are usually four to six narrower lanceolate leaves in a basal rosette. Occurs in the eastern Mediterranean area. Both species are worth cultivating and present no problems in a sunny border.

A. protensum See *A. schubertii*.

A. pulchellum Similar to *A. flavum* and differing most obviously in the purple flowers. Umbels with many flowers which are at first pendent and later erect, in the fruiting stage. Each flower is small and bell-shaped. There is a good white form which appears to breed true from seed. It is a charming, mid-summer species and seeds freely, therefore being very suitable as a garden plant for informal layouts. It occurs in south and south-east Europe.

A. regelii One of the most extraordinary species since it has an inflorescence consisting of several whorls of flowers one above the other like a 'candelabra' primula. It grows up to 100cm in height with a few basal leaves up to 5cm wide, which usually die away by flowering time. The whorls of flowers are up to six in number, the lowest being 8–10cm in diameter, the rest becoming progressively smaller towards the apex. The individual flowers are papery in texture, 1–1·5cm in diameter, pale whitish-lilac with a darker stripe along the centre of each segment. *A. regelii* occurs in north-east Iran, Afghanistan and Russian Central Asia.

A. rosenbachianum One of the most well-known of the tall purple-flowered species, growing up to 100cm in height with a dense 10cm diameter spherical umbel of small starry flowers. The perianth segments are narrow and soon shrivel up and reflex, leaving the stamens protruding prominently. Leaves 1–5cm wide, glaucous. Grows wild in Afghanistan, Baluchistan and Russian Tadjikistan in stony hills up to 3500m altitude. *A. jesdianum* from northern Iraq and western Iran is very similar to this and differs mainly in having a fibrous, netted bulb coat whereas that of *A. rosenbachianum* is papery. *A. suwarowii* is also similar, but has a tougher papery tunic to its bulb and smaller flowers (segments 4–5mm long) than in *A. rosenbachianum* (segments 6–10mm long). All of these species need a warm well-drained position to succeed well.

A. roseum A handsome plant, but care should be taken to select a good colour form which does not produce bulblets in amongst the flowers as these forms are less attractive and can be very weedy. Stem 25–40cm high with 5–7cm umbels of bright-pink flowers, each 1–1·5cm diameter. The segments are broad and overlapping, giving a substantial flower. The few narrow leaves on the lower part of the stem disappear before or at flowering time. Common in Mediterranean regions at low altitudes in grassy places and areas of old cultivation. In mild districts in southern England it is a good garden plant but in very favoured areas such as the south-west and southern United States it should perhaps be avoided since it might do rather too well!

A. schubertii An unusual species, having enormous umbels up to 25cm in diameter on stems 40–60cm in height. The umbels are made up of pedicels of very unequal lengths from 4cm to 20cm long, so that although there are many flowers the whole inflorescence looks rather loose. Flowers pale rose, 1·5cm in diameter. The leaves are basal and broadly linear. Occurs from Syria to Israel in fields at low altitudes and is not very hardy in Britain. A bulb frame or cold greenhouse gives the best chance of success. *A. protensum* is rather similar in having the unequal pedicels but is a smaller plant occurring in northern Afghanistan and Russian Central Asia.

A. siculum See genus *Nectaroscordum*.

A. sphaerocephalum A slender species of no great garden value but quite useful in a wild garden for naturalizing in borders. Grows up to 60cm in height with a few very narrow scattered leaves on the lower third of the stem. The umbel is about 2–3cm diameter, very tight, with many small bell-shaped, pinkish-purple flowers with protruding style and stamens. Very widespread in Europe and western Asia.

A. stipitatum See *A. hirtifolium*.

A. suwarowii See *A. rosenbachianum*.

A. victorialis A rather unusual-looking species with tufts of erect netted bulb-like rhizomes and a leafy stem up to 40cm in height. The leaves are elliptical up to about 6cm wide and are narrowed to a sheath at the base. The umbel is 3–5cm in diameter, very dense with small white flowers. Widespread from central Europe to the Himalayas in woods and alpine pastures. Not very striking but interesting because of its unusual appearance.

Amaryllis Amaryllidaceae

Although the large-flowered South American *Hippeastrum* species and hybrids are often popularly referred to as Amaryllis, the name really applies to a South African monotypic genus. This one species, *A. belladonna*, is a well-known plant for it flowers in autumn and is hardy in countries as far north as Britain and is a beautiful, exotic plant for a late display. The large bulbs are best planted in a warm position, the best groups I have ever seen being along the sunny side of a greenhouse where the reflected light in summer raised the soil temperature considerably. Any warm border will do and the ground should be kept clean from weeds or other plants which would shade the resting bulbs in summer. The whole secret of flowering *A. belladonna* is to give the bulbs as hot and dry conditions as possible during their rest. An annual dressing of bonemeal in late summer is beneficial. In cold areas, a pane of glass or light scattering of dry bracken is sufficient to prevent frost damage to the leaves, which remain green from late autumn to early summer. Propagation is by division of established clumps of bulbs.

A. belladonna The purplish flowering stems reach 45–90cm in height, emerging before the leaves appear. The umbel has a spread of about 15–25cm, the number of flowers varying enormously from two or three to up to 30 in some cultivated varieties, although I have never actually seen a specimen with that many. Each flower is rather funnel-shaped with a short perianth tube, about 10cm in length and 10–15cm in diameter, normally bright-pink, but white and darker forms exist; they are delicately scented and in the wild attract hawk-moths. The strap-shaped leaves are 1–2cm wide, produced after flowering, in a fan-like basal tuft alongside the old flowering shoot. Flowering September–November in Britain. Occurs wild in the south-west Cape region on coastal hills and stream banks among bushes, although it appears to flower best after a fire has destroyed the undergrowth.

Cultivars of *A. belladonna* include 'Hathor' (white); 'Kewensis' (very vigorous; throat of flower yellowish); 'Rubra' (deeper pink-red than is usual); 'Parkeri' (many flowers to each umbel, possibly *Amaryllis* × *Brunsvigia*); 'Windhoek' (pink with white centre); 'Cape Town' (deep rose-red).

In addition to *A. belladonna* and its variants, there are now several intergeneric hybrids between it and *Nerine bowdenii* (× *Amarine*); *Amaryllis* × *Crinum moorei* (× *Amarcrinum* or × *Crinodonna*) and *Brunsvigia josephinae* × *Amaryllis belladonna* (× *Brunsdonna*). Although these are all beautiful plants they do not, to my mind, add anything to their parent, the Belladonna Lily.

Arisaema Araceae

Curious tuberous-rooted plants in the Arum family which deserve to be more widely cultivated. They do not have the disagreeable odour which is the disadvantage of many members of the family. Although a large genus, very few have been tried in Britain, which is a pity because many of the Chinese and Japanese species should be hardy. There are, for example, 42 species recognized for Japan alone and I know of only two of these which are in cultivation here. They have very small insignificant flowers, densely arranged on a pencil-like spadix which is surrounded by the large hood-like spathe. This often has a long tail-like appendage at its apex and is usually greenish or purplish in colour. The leaves are deeply lobed. In my experience Arisaemas are always very late emerging from the ground, often into June.

A. candidissimum This is by far the best species for British gardens. It is about 30cm in height when in full leaf, but the inflorescences are produced before the large three-lobed leaves expand. Each spathe is about 8–10cm long on a 15cm stem and is tubular with an expanded hood over the apex, and a short 2·5cm 'tail'. The colour is white with either pinkish suffusion and striping or with a greenish tinge. The spadix is white or creamy-yellow. It is a native of western China.

I have tried this in several situations and it seems to be happy wherever it is planted, in sun or semi-shade, in damp or dry situations and in heavy or light soils. My best attempts, however, have always been in warm sunny places, such as a south-facing wall can provide. It increases freely by offset tubers.

A. consanguineum An easily-grown species suitable for peat or woodland gardens. The stem grows up to 100cm in height and is greenish with beautiful mottling in brown, carrying, umbrella-like, a much divided palmate leaf and a green, brownish-purple striped, 15–18cm long spathe in summer. The fruit is a cluster of red berries held in a pendulous position. I have grown this for several years now from some seed given to me by Desmond Meikle. It is certainly hardy in south-west England and mine has survived hard frosts in Surrey, so it is probably hardier than is usually reported. It is a native of western China.

A. griffithii A beautiful species which has proved to be hardy in my peat garden. The leaves are three-lobed, with the green broadly-ovate lobes outlined with crimson. The spathe is rather wide and about 15cm long, greenish with purple veining and spotting. It occurs wild in the Himalayas.

A. sikokianum One of the most dramatic species, but I have not tried it yet although it is obtainable from some nurseries. The spathe is deep brown-purple, about 15cm long, and the large spadix is white and club-shaped, protruding from the tube and contrasting well with the colour of the spathe. The leaf has three to five broadly-obovate toothed leaflets. It is a native of Japan.

A. triphyllum This is an easily-grown species and prefers the peat garden or a shaded site among shrubs. The leaves are three-lobed and the green spathe is about 10cm in length, hooded over at the apex, which has led to the common name of 'Jack-in-the-Pulpit'. It occurs wild in the eastern United States. Seed is produced in Britain and the clusters of red berries are quite ornamental in autumn.

Bloomeria Liliaceae

A small genus, related to *Brodiaea* and *Triteleia*, which is not at all well known in gardens. A discussion about its botanical characteristics can be found under the genus *Brodiaea*, and the cultural requirements are the same. The height is usually 20–30cm.

B. crocea This is confused with *Triteleia crocea* (*Brodiaea crocea*) and *T. ixioides* as they all have yellow flowers. However, the generic feature of the cup-like base to the filaments clearly separates *Bloomeria* from the other two. It has many flowers in an umbel up to 15cm in diameter. The flowers are 1·5–2cm in diameter with a very short perianth tube, and are yellow with a dark stripe along the centre of each segment. It grows wild in California in open places up to 2300m.

Bravoa Agavaceae

A small central American genus named after Nicholas Bravo, a hero of the Mexican Independence. It is related to *Polianthes* and included in that genus by some authorities, although the three species usually included in *Bravoa* have red or orange flowers and in this way differ from the white or greenish-flowered *Polianthes*. Almost certainly none of the species is completely hardy and my own experience is that they need a cool greenhouse not falling below 10°C in winter when the plants are dormant. The tubers can alternatively be lifted and stored in a warm place in winter. In spring they can be planted into greenhouse beds or in large pots, but in either case must be given a rich well-drained soil for they are strong-growing plants. They must be re-potted annually or fed with a slow-acting general fertilizer.

B. geminiflora (*Polianthes geminiflora*) has a bulbous rootstock with a tuft of thick fibres at the apex. Leaves lanceolate, mostly basal, glabrous, glaucous green, 0·5–2cm wide and 15–35cm long. The inflorescence is rather loose and raceme-like and reaches 30–70cm with a few small scattered leaves on the lower portion. The coral or yellow flowers are produced in pairs on short pedicels in the axils of bracts and are narrowly funnel-shaped with a 2–2·5cm long tube, only 7mm across at the mouth, which is bent abruptly just above the base so that the flower is horizontal or slightly deflexed. The lobes are less than 5mm long. Flowering June–July in Britain. Central Mexico, in damp places from 1500–2800m.

My plants were grown from seed collected by Sally Walker at 2300m in Tapalpa and from this altitude may be fairly hardy. The seed germinates well and grows into flowering-sized tubers in only two years.

B. graminifolia (*Polianthes graminifolia*) is similar to *B. geminiflora* but has very narrow grassy leaves, hairy below. The flowers are deeper red. Central Mexico, in meadows.

B. platyphylla (*Polianthes platyphylla*) as its name suggests has broad leaves, ovate in shape, 1·2–3cm broad, 7–13cm long and lying flat on the ground, and a few scattered bract-like stem leaves. Flowers less than 2cm long (at least 2cm in the other species), pale red, with the stamens attached near the top of the tube (near the base in the other two species). Central Mexico.

Brodiaea Liliaceae

This is one of a group of closely related genera from America having corms with fibrous tunics and umbellate *Allium*-like inflorescences. The other major genera involved in the group are *Triteleia*, *Bloomeria*, *Dichelostemma* and *Muilla*. Various species of the first three genera are cultivated to some extent, but *Muilla* (which is *Allium* spelt backwards!) is little known in British gardens and is of no great garden value. *M. maritima* is in some collections and is a fairly dwarf species with a dense tuft of narrow leaves and an umbel of small yellow starry flowers.

The five genera may be separated as follows:

A	Proper stamens three, the other three flattened and not carrying anthers	B
	Proper stamens six, all carrying anthers	C
B	Leaves rounded beneath; stigma 3-lobed	*Brodiaea*
	Leaves with an angular keel beneath; stigma nearly entire	*Dichelostemma*
C	Leaves with an angular keel beneath	D
	Leaves with a rounded underside	*Muilla*
D	Filaments of the stamens cup-like at the base	*Bloomeria*
	Filaments flattened at base with no cup	*Triteleia*

Brodiaeas are not very exciting plants on the whole, but a few of the species are quite useful as they flower in early summer in Britain when most bulbs have finished. They present no problems in cultivation and are hardy in the south, at least, requiring only a sheltered sunny border in well-drained soil. I have grown them quite satisfactorily among clumps of *Iris stylosa* where they get some protection from the *Iris* leaves in winter. All the species have more or less linear leaves which are produced very early so that by flowering time they have almost died away. The larger-flowered species can be quite useful for dried-flower arrangements. Many of the former *Brodiaea* species have now been transferred to the other genera in the group.

B. bridgesii See *Triteleia bridgesii*.

B. californica A large-flowered species with a substantial umbel of up to 15 flowers about 30–40cm in length when in flower. The flowers are funnel-shaped,

3–4cm long and 2·5–3cm in diameter at the mouth, and rather variable in colour from white to pale pink to deep purplish-blue, usually with a darker mid-vein to each segment. The three sterile stamens are very obvious, being flat and whitish. It grows wild in stony or gritty grassy places in California.

B. coccinea See *Dichelostemma ida-maia*.

B. coronaria This grows 20–30cm in height and has a few-flowered umbel with the individual flowers 2·5–3cm long and 1·5–2cm in diameter at the mouth, deep purple-blue. The three sterile stamens are flat and yellowish or cream. A pink-flowered form is known. It is widely distributed in the western states of North America, from British Columbia south to California, in dry rocky and grassy places.

B. grandiflora See *Triteleia grandiflora*.

B. hyacinthina See *Triteleia hyacinthina*.

B. ida-maia See *Dichelostemma ida-maia*.

B. ixioides See *Triteleia ixioides*.

B. laxa See *Triteleia laxa*.

B. minor A slender species, very variable in height from 5–25cm. The umbel carries two to 12 pinkish or lilac-blue flowers 1·5–2cm long and 1·5cm in diameter at the mouth. The perianth tube is constricted above the ovary where the lobes begin. It occurs wild in California on rocky slopes up to 400m altitude.

B. pulchella See *Dichelostemma pulchella*.

B. × tubergenii See *Triteleia × tubergenii*.

B. volubilis See *Dichelostemma volubile*.

Calochortus Liliaceae

A genus of almost 60 species which occur wild in western America from British Columbia south to Mexico. They are among the most beautiful of all the spring and summer bulbs but very few are in cultivation in Britain. Since first trying them about ten years ago I have slowly become more confident in trying them outdoors, and in my present garden in Surrey I am very encouraged by the results. The success has mainly been with *C. albus* which is one of the easier species. It is planted in a sandy soil between heathers in a position which dries out in summer because of many tree roots, although the site is not actually over-hung by branches. Initially I grew them in pots where their rather lanky habit made them somewhat out of place and not at all attractive. The bulb frame is probably ideal, for they like the unrestricted root-run, and the spring watering and summer baking they require can be controlled by the use of frame-lights. Once they have become dormant in summer they can be kept dry through autumn and winter until the first watering in early spring. Propagation is mainly by seed which takes up to four years to flower. Some species produce aerial bulblets in the axils of the leaves and a few produce offset bulblets underground.

The local names of *Calochortus* are often very descriptive, such as Cat's Ears,

Mariposa Lily or Tulip, Globe Lily, Fairy Lantern and Golden Lantern. Botanically there are three fairly distinct sections, Eucalochortus, Mariposa and Cyclobothra. The last is sometimes split off as a separate genus. The Eucalochortus have orbicular to oblong, winged capsules; while the other two groups have elongated fruits without wings. Mariposa and Cyclobothra differ in their bulb tunics, the former having papery coats, often ribbed lengthways, while the latter has netted, fibrous tunics. *Fritillaria* is about the nearest genus in appearance but even this is not very closely related. The three outer perianth segments are usually smaller than the inner and are rather sepal-like, while the inner are large and showy and have a sunken gland, the shape of which is often taxonomically important.

There is a revision of the genus by M. Ownbey in *Annals of the Missouri Botanical Garden* vol. 27 (1940).

The species mentioned mostly have linear stem leaves, sometimes with one basal leaf. The letters E, M or C denote Eucalochortus, Mariposa or Cyclobothra.

C. albus (E) This grows up to 30cm in height with several pendulous, globular, white to pinkish-red lantern-like flowers, 2–3cm long and wide. The outer segments are acute and much smaller than the rounded inner segments which are fringed and lined with hairs. The pinkish forms are called var. *rubellus*. It is common in the Sierra Nevada and coast ranges of California up to 500m altitude. Flowering May–June in Britain. *C. albus* is one of the easier species in cultivation, flowering well and setting seed freely.

C. amabilis (E) A rather similar plant to *C. albus* in its general appearance, but it has deep-yellow flowers 2–2·5cm long with the outer segments often brownish-tinted. It grows wild in the northern coast ranges of California among pines and oaks up to 400m altitude. Flowering June–July.

C. amoenus (E) This is rather like *C. albus* but has rose-purple flowers and the gland is very broad, occupying an area which extends to the edges of the inner segments, whereas in *C. albus* it is small and only in the middle of each segment. It is a lovely plant, occurring wild in California in the Sierra Nevada mountains at up to 500m in slight shade. Flowering June–July.

C. barbatus (C) (*Cyclobothra barbata*, *C. lutea*, *Calochortus flavus* but not *Calochortus luteus* q.v.) This is a perfectly easy and hardy species in Britain in spite of being one of the most southern in its distribution. It will do well in a warm sunny border where it flowers in late summer. It increases very well by bulbils, produced in the leaf axils. The flowers are pendent, campanulate, about 2–3cm in diameter, and are deep mustard-yellow with the segments fringed and lined with long hairs. The outside of the flower is sometimes purplish. It grows wild in Mexico at up to 2500m in grassy places or in slight shade of oaks. Flowering July–September in Britain.

C. clavatus (M) A vigorous species 20–30cm in height with an umbellate or branched inflorescence of huge yellow erect flowers about 6cm in diameter,

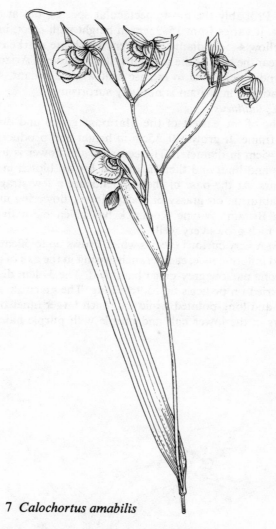

7 *Calochortus amabilis*

sometimes with brownish outer segments. The much larger inner segments have hairs on their inner surface. It grows wild in California in the southern Sierra Nevada and southern Coast Ranges at up to 800m in clearings and on open slopes among rocks.

C. ghiesebrechtii (C) A beautiful species although not as large-flowered as many of the Calochortus species. The flowers are erect, widely campanulate and purplish with all the segments hairy on their inner surfaces and more or less equal in size. It grows in Mexico and Guatemala in the mountains at up to 2800m altitude.

C. kennedyi (M) Probably the most spectacular species, but at the same time the most difficult. It varies from 15–35cm in height with erect, intense orange-scarlet, red or yellow 4–5cm diameter flowers which are marked with a purple or black blotch near the base of the segments. It is a native of Arizona and south-east California and is subjected to intense heat when dormant, so that lack of success in cultivating it in Britain is not very surprising.

C. lilacinus See *C. uniflorus*.

C. luteus (M) One of the easiest of the Mariposa group and doing extremely well in my bulb frame. It grows 20–35cm in height and produces erect bright-yellow flowers 4–5cm in diameter. The centre of the flower is usually marked with brown dots and lines and there is often a brown blotch in the middle of the inner segments. At the base of the segments are a few straggling hairs. It grows wild in California on grassy or rocky slopes, flowering in May or June in cultivation in Britain. Wayne Roderick has given me a fine rich-yellow-coloured form which grows very well.

C. obispoensis (E) A very curious species which grows up to 50cm in height with a much-branched inflorescence, each branch arising in the axil of a reduced stem leaf. It has one long narrow grey-green basal leaf. The 3–4cm diameter flowers are erect and carried on pedicels up to 9cm long. The greenish outer segments are very narrow and long-pointed while the much larger inner ones are yellow with yellow hairs in the lower half and purple with purple hairs in the upper

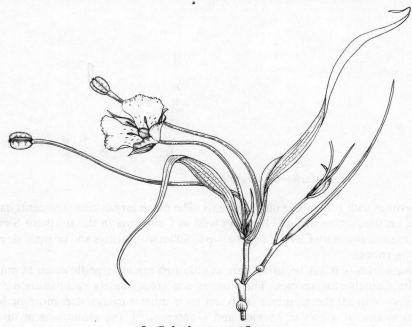

8 *Calochortus uniflorus*

half. The gland shows up as a dense tuft of long deep-yellow hairs, and the stamens have yellow filaments and coffee-coloured anthers. In Britain it flowers in June. It is a native of California, in San Luis Obispo county.

C. pulchellus (E) An easy and very attractive species with several yellow, globose, nodding flowers in a branched but compact inflorescence. They are about 3cm in length and width, rather larger than the otherwise similar *C. amabilis*, and are even more globose than in that species. It is a native of California in the Mount Diablo area among pines and oaks.

C. uniflorus (E) One of the easiest species to grow in Britain and it might grow well in a raised bed outside, although I have only tried it in a bulb frame to date. It does need full sun and the bed should be in a warm situation. It grows to 25cm in height with several lilac flowers on long pedicels, in an umbel. They are erect, 4–5cm in diameter and have a dark spot in the centre of each inner segment. The segments have very few hairs present on the inside. It grows wild in California and south-west Oregon in dampish pastures. Flowers May–June in Britain. It can be increased by stem bulbils.

C. venustus (M) One of the very showy large-flowered species, 15–40cm in height. The erect flowers are open-bowl shaped, up to 6cm in diameter, and very variable in colour from cream to yellow, purplish or reddish. The centre of the flower is marked by a deep-red blotch at the base of each segment. It occurs in California in the Sierra Nevada and the coast ranges in gritty or sandy soils up to 2400m altitude. The cream form is the easiest to grow in Britain in my experience. *C. vestae* is rather similar to this.

C. weedii (C) Although a Cyclobothra, this has erect flowers more like a Mariposa. The inflorescence contains several flowers, each 4–5cm in diameter, yellow with brown lines and speckling. The inner segments are covered with long hairs on the inside, while the outer segments are very narrowly acute. It grows in California on rocky hillsides.

Camassia Liliaceae

An entirely American genus comprised of five species from North America – the bulbs of which used to be eaten by some Indian tribes – and one South American species, formerly a separate genus *Fortunatia*. They are bulbous plants with long linear basal leaves and a racemose inflorescence which usually bears large, rather starry, white, blue or violet flowers, although in *C. biflora* they are small and whitish. Camassias are perhaps best likened to a large *Scilla*, a genus entirely absent from the Americas. Most species are native to damp grassland and in cultivation they present no problems here in Britain. In fact they do well planted in grass and I once grew them successfully in some rough turf under apple trees where they looked most attractive in early summer.

In dealing with the genus I have mainly followed Gould in *The American Midland Naturalist* of November 1942. The main features used in distinguishing the species are the colour, whether or not the flowers are regular in shape and the position of the perianth segments when they wither. In some species they remain joined together, covering the capsule, while in others they shrivel away separately so that the developing capsule is not covered. The disposition of the pedicels (i.e. the flower stalks) is important, whether or not they are horizontal or erect.

C. angusta A synonym of *C. scilloides.*

C. biflora The only South American species, formerly in the genus *Fortunatia.* It was called 'biflora' because it frequently produces two flowers per bract, but it can vary from one to three (hence one of the synonyms is *Fortunatia triflora*). It is not a very attractive plant, reaching 40–50cm with a loose raceme of flowers, each about 1–1·5cm in diameter on a pedicel up to 4cm long. The leaves are basal, as long or longer than the inflorescence and about 1cm wide. The flattish flowers are rather *Scilla*-like in appearance and are white or pinkish-purple outside with a purple vein along the centre of each segment. It occurs in Peru, Bolivia, Paraguay, Chile and Argentina from 50–3000m in dry rocky places or in scrub on hills. This is in cultivation in Britain from plants collected by Miss Pamela Holt in Peru and by David Cutler in Argentina. It flowers here between October and May but is not hardy and needs temperate greenhouse conditions.

C. cusickii This grows 50–80cm in height with slightly shorter, rather succulent, linear basal leaves 2–4cm wide; pedicels 1·5–3cm long, horizontal or turning upwards. Flowers pale to deep violet-blue, slightly irregular in shape with the segments 2·5–3·5cm long, shrivelling away separately from each other (see above). North-east Oregon in the Wallowa Mountains where it is said to grow on hillsides rather than in wet meadows, which is the most common habitat for Camassias.

C. fraseri A synonym of *C. scilloides.*

C. howellii Up to 100cm in height with basal leaves about 0·5–1cm wide; pedicels 1·5–2·5cm long, spreading horizontally. Flowers deep violet-blue, regular in shape with segments 1–2cm long, joining together over the young capsule as they shrivel. Occurs in a small area of south-west Oregon in meadows.

C. hyacinthina A synonym of *C. scilloides.*

C. leichtlinii Can reach 130cm in height with basal leaves much shorter and about 0·5–2·5cm wide; pedicels 1·5–5cm long, directed upwards a little. Flowers very variable in colour from deep blue-violet to white, or rarely pinkish, regular in shape with the perianth segments 2–5cm long, joining together over the young capsule on shrivelling. Widespread in the wild from Vancouver Island south to the Sierra Nevada range, mostly in meadows above 600m. Two subspecies are recognized: (a) subsp. *typica*, with creamy-white flowers and (b) subsp. *suksdorfii* with flowers varying from blue to violet. The white form is occasionally offered in nurseries as 'var. alba'. A semi-double is known as 'forma plena' or 'var. semiplena' and a very deep purple one has been named 'var. atroviolacea'.

C. scilloides Grows 25–80cm in height with 0·5–2cm wide leaves often nearly as long as the inflorescence; pedicels 0·5–3cm long turned upwards from the horizontal. Flowers regular, varying violet-blue to white, the segments 0·5–1·5cm long, usually shrivelling separately without covering the ovary. Widespread in the eastern and southern states of North America in grassland or light woodland.

C. quamash (*C. esculenta*, *C. teapeae*) A very variable species, so much so that as many as seven subspecies have been recognized. It varies 20–80cm in height with leaves 0·5–2cm broad, nearly as long as the inflorescence, green to very greyish green on the upper surface; pedicels 0·5–3cm long, spreading horizontally or erect and incurved especially at fruiting stage. Flowers pale blue to deep violet-blue or white, regular and irregular flowers usually mixed on the same raceme; segments 1–3·5cm long, either shrivelling away separately or remaining joined over the capsule. Widespread in the western states from British Columbia south to California and east as far as Montana and Utah. It grows in various situations from dry hills to very wet meadows or light woodland, up to 1700m altitude.

The subspecies are:

(a) subsp. *maxima* Leaves 0·5–1·5cm wide, slightly greyish on upper surface; pedicels horizontal or erect; flowers deep blue-violet; segments 0·5–1cm wide and 2–3·5cm long.

(b) subsp. *quamash* (subsp. *typica*) Leaves greyish-green on upper surface, 0·5–2cm wide; pedicels erect in fruit; flowers pale to deep blue or blue-violet; segments 0·3–0·5cm wide and 1·5–3cm long.

(c) subsp. *azurea* Leaves 0·5–1·3cm wide, slightly greyish on upper surface; pedicels horizontal even in fruit; flowers light blue-violet; segments 0·1–0·3cm wide and 2–3·5cm long.

(d) subsp. *intermedia* Leaves 0·5–1·3cm wide, green on both sides; pedicels erect in fruit; flowers pale blue-violet; segments 0·3–0·5cm wide, 2–3·5cm long.

(e) subsp. *walpolei* Leaves 0·4–1·3cm wide, green on both surfaces; pedicels erect in fruit; flowers pale blue or blue-violet; segments 0·3–0·5cm wide, 1·2–2cm long.

(f) subsp. *linearis* Leaves green on both surfaces, 0·5–1·5cm wide; pedicels erect in fruit; flowers deep violet-blue; segments 0·5–0·8cm wide, 2–3·5cm long.

(g) subsp. *breviflora* Leaves grey-green on upper surface, 1–1·7cm wide; pedicels erect in fruit; flowers blue to deep blue-violet; segments 0·3–0·5cm wide, 1·5–2cm long.

(h) subsp. *utahensis* Leaves grey on upper surface, pedicels erect in fruit; flowers usually pale blue-violet; segments 0·3–0·6cm wide, 2–3cm long.

Cardiocrinum Liliaceae

A small, eastern Asiatic genus related to *Lilium* and differing in having large heart-shaped leaves and a monocarpic bulb, that is one which dies after flowering. Additionally, the capsule has very noticeable teeth along the edges of the compartments when it splits open. They are woodland plants and are not difficult to grow, given a deep layer of leafmould and cool moist conditions. The large bulbs, which take many years to reach flowering size, should be planted near to the surface. After flowering, the parent bulb dies and produces several offsets which take about three to four years to flower – rather more rapidly than from seed which can be as much as seven years. They all flower in late summer in Britain.

C. cathayanum This grows up to 130cm in height and has a group of about six oblong-ovate long-petioled leaves one-third or half-way up the stem, but none below this and only a few smaller ones above. The flowers, one to five in number, are funnel-shaped and 10–13cm in length, greenish-white on the outside and cream-white inside. It is the least showy species of the genus and is a native of east and central China.

C. cordatum A larger species, 120–180cm in height, which has widely-cordate leaves up to 30cm in length with a long petiole. These are usually scattered on the stem from about half-way, upwards. The four to 15 flowers are creamy-white trumpets, up to 15cm long, marked with yellow blotching inside and some brownish spotting. It grows wild in Japan, the Kuriles and on Sakhalin.

C. giganteum This is by far the most spectacular and the easiest of the three to grow in Britain, growing to a height of 180–250cm with a rosette of huge, ovate, cordate basal leaves of a rich deep green, the blade being up to 50cm long. The stem leaves are alternate and rather smaller. The inflorescence consists of a raceme of about ten to 25 slightly downward-pointing scented flowers which are huge white funnels about 15cm in length. Inside, the segments are purplish-striped and the exterior is sometimes tinted greenish. *C. giganteum* occurs in the Himalayas through Nepal to southern Tibet and northern Burma.

In China there is a variant known as var. *yunnanense* which has bronze-coloured foliage and is slightly smaller with horizontal flowers. There are no purple marks on the inside of the segments. *C. giganteum* is best grown in very rich soil with a lot of organic matter such as well-rotted manure. In cold winters the bulbs should be covered with a layer of bracken for protection. The best site is in a cool glade among rhododendrons where there is dappled sunlight.

Crinum Amaryllidaceae

A mainly tropical and subtropical genus of rather exotic-looking plants, only one or two of which can be classed as hardy in Britain. There are probably something in the region of 100 species in South America, Africa, India, southeast Asia and Australia but it is the more temperate South African species which have been the most useful, since several are summer-rainfall plants and have adapted quite well to cultivation in milder parts of England. Crinums mostly have very large bulbs, often shaped like Indian clubs. These give rise to tufts of usually rather fleshy leaves, either all in one plane (distichous) or in a rosette. The stout inflorescence arises next to the leafy shoot, not from its centre, and carries an umbel of large, often wide to narrow funnel-shaped flowers which have a long perianth tube and six equal segments.

C. bulbispermum A robust species up to 90cm in height with grey-green leaves up to 10cm wide, in a rosette. The umbel has between five and 15 sweetly-scented flowers which are funnel-shaped, white or pinkish with a reddish keel along the centre of each segment. The perianth tube is 6–10cm long and the free part of the segments 9–10cm long. It grows wild in the Transvaal, the Orange Free State, Natal and Lesotho in damp places near streams. I have seen this growing very well in a garden in Wiltshire, a most handsome clump-forming species which is very suitable for the herbaceous border.

C. moorei A beautiful species worthy of more widespread recognition as a good garden plant for the milder British gardens. It grows up to 100cm in height with a rosette of broad green leaves, 8–12cm wide. The umbel is five- to ten-flowered and each flower is pink, or more rarely white, with no red keel to the segments. The perianth tube is 8–10cm long and the segments about the same length. Although the shape is funnel-like, the flower is very wide open since the segments spread out abruptly, giving a diameter of about 15–20cm. It occurs in damp marshy places and streamsides in Natal and the eastern Cape.

C. × powellii This is the hybrid between *C. moorei* and *C. bulbispermum* which is a better and hardier garden plant than either of its parents. It grows from 60 to 100cm in height and has bright green leaves in a rosette. The umbel contains five to ten trumpet-shaped pink flowers which are usually arched over with a curving perianth tube and are about 10cm across at the mouth. The segments recurve somewhat at their tips. It flowers in late summer, in August and September, and is easily grown in a warm sunny situation where it is best left undisturbed, for not only does it take some time to settle in but also the bulbs are so colossal that it is too much effort to move them. They can measure as much as 20cm in diameter and up to 90cm in length. Offsets are produced and will grow quite rapidly to form sizeable clumps of bulbs. My main objection to the plant is its rather tatty foliage which always looks as if it has been damaged by frost. A pure white form is known and if planted with a dark background is more effective than the pink form.

Crocosmia Iridaceae

A southern African genus, most well-known because of the Montbretia which is a hybrid between *C. aurea* and *C. pottsii*. The former is a tender plant in British gardens, with panicles of orange flowers up to 90cm in height and a fan of broad Iris-like leaves on the lower part of the inflorescence. *C. pottsii* is similar with yellow, red-flushed flowers. Neither species is cultivated very much. Crocosmias have flowers with a long perianth tube and six short spreading perianth segments.

The leaves are produced in a flattish fan with the inflorescence arising terminally from the centre of the fan. They are easily propagated, for the corms increase quite rapidly and can be divided during the dormant period, preferably in early spring. In Britain Crocosmias flower in late summer.

C. × *crocosmiiflora* This is the name which covers all the Montbretia hybrids originating from *C. aurea* × *C. pottsii*. There are many cultivars varying in flower colour from yellow to orange and reddish. They are mostly 60–100cm in height and are vigorous and useful garden plants, although in mild districts they can be too successful and have become naturalized in many places.

C. masonorum A rather stately plant about 80cm in height with broad pleated leaves in a fan. The 2–3cm long flowers are produced in dense arching panicles and are bright orange with long protruding stamens. *C. masonorum* is a native of the Cape and flowers in July and August in Britain. It requires a warm sunny border and in cold winters should be protected with bracken or coarse peat placed over the dormant corms.

Curtonus Iridaceae

C. paniculatus is a splendid late-summer-flowering plant from the eastern Cape, Natal and Transvaal, which grows up to 120cm in height with a fan of broad Iris-like pleated leaves. The inflorescence is open-branched and carries many long-tubular orange-red flowers up to 5cm in length which have rather short, unequal, perianth segments. The corms increase well and can be divided up in autumn or early spring for replanting immediately in a sunny well-drained soil. *Curtonus* is a monotypic genus related to *Crocosmia* (Montbretia).

Cypella Iridaceae

South American bulbs, not unlike *Tigridia*. Most of the species have brightly-coloured short-lived flowers in succession, these having an *Iris*-like appearance with three large outer perianth segments and three smaller inner ones. The style branches are, however, not large and showy ('petaloid') as in *Iris*. In countries with frosty winters, they are not hardy and should be lifted and stored in a frost-free shed or greenhouse, preferably in sand so that the bulbs do not dry out excessively. *C. herbertii* is one of the hardiest and will survive and thrive in southern England. Seed is normally produced freely and the seedlings flower in their second or third year.

C. herbertii Grows 30–50cm in height with a few long linear leaves. Inflorescence usually much-branched with many flowers in succession from the green bracts. Flowers 4–6cm in diameter, with the three large spreading outer segments a dullish mustard-yellow; inner three much smaller, inrolled, yellow spotted with purple. Anthers and style purplish. Grows in Uruguay and Argentina in damp grassy places. Flowers in August in Britain and is the easiest species. It prefers warm borders and will seed itself among low shrubs.

9 *Curtonus paniculatus*

C. herbertii var. *brevicristata* is to my mind an improvement since it has bright lemon yellow coloured flowers, but is of less vigorous growth.
C. herrerae 20–40cm in height without or with few branches to the stem and with a few narrow leaves near the base; stem leaves much shorter with bulbils in the axils. Flowers several in succession, 5–6cm in diameter, the outer segments larger than the inner and spreading, deep blue; the inner segments more erect and recurved at the tips, blue with a bright yellow crest in the centre. The central

portion of the flower, forming the cup, is white with reddish-brown spotting. Occurs wild in Peru in grass and rocky places at 3500–4500m. Flowering in December in Britain, so requires a frost-free greenhouse. This beautiful plant came to me a few years ago and proved easy to grow, increasing by the stem bulbils, but unfortunately I lost it during a dry summer spell when the bulbs became over-dried. Coming from such an altitude it probably does not require too much baking during its dormancy.

C. peruviana Stem 20–60cm in height with a few pleated leaves 1–2·5cm wide and an often unbranched inflorescence with a succession of flowers from within the bracts. Sometimes, in vigorous specimens, the upper leaf axils also produce inflorescences. Flowers brilliant deep yellow, erect, 5–7cm in diameter, flattish, the three outer segments with an orbicular blade, the inner three much smaller and inrolled, furnished with a mass of hairs on the curved portion. The lower part of each segment forming the cup is banded with purple spots. Wild in Peru at 850–3300m on moist, sometimes mossy banks and grassy places. Flowers in winter in Britain and can only be grown in a cool greenhouse.

C. plumbea The Blue Tiger Lily. A robust plant, 40–75cm in height when in flower, with several flat basal leaves up to 2cm wide. Inflorescence unbranched, the large green spathes producing several 6–8cm diameter flowers in succession. These are blue with brownish shading and spotting in the cup at the base of the segments. Near the centre of the three smaller segments is a yellow patch. Occurs wild in Brazil and Uruguay, flowering in late summer in Britain. A beautiful vigorous species which grows very well in my cool greenhouse, planted out, where it has made a large clump. It is not hardy outdoors but could be lifted for the winter months.

Dichelostemma Liliaceae

This belongs to a group of genera from North America, related to *Allium* in having an umbellate inflorescence. They are placed by some taxonomists in Amaryllidaceae because of this feature, but others treat them to a separate family, Alliaceae. Since opinion varies so much I have left them in Liliaceae, for they have six stamens (although three of them are sometimes sterile) and a superior ovary, in keeping with the rest of Liliaceae. *Dichelostemma* and *Brodiaea* differ from the other related genera, *Triteleia*, *Bloomeria* and *Muilla*, in usually having three fertile stamens instead of six. The leaves and style distinguish between the other two, *Dichelostemma* having leaves strongly keeled beneath and an indistinctly lobed stigma, while *Brodiaea* has leaves rounded beneath and a three-lobed stigma.

Dichelostemmas, about six species altogether, come from the western states of North America and have proved to be hardy in Surrey, although may well be rather tender farther to the north. They need plenty of sun and good drainage and I find that they are flowering particularly well in the spring following the

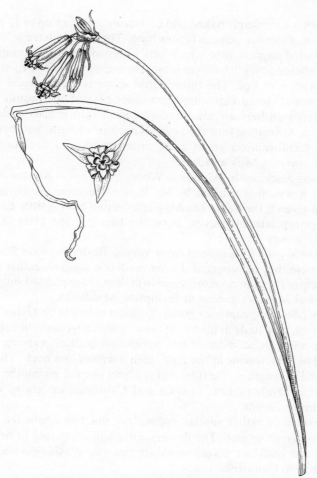

10 *Dichelostemma ida-maia*

hot summer of 1976. It is therefore reasonable to assume that in a cool damp summer it would be best to cover the bulbs with a pane of glass to warm up the soil, or grow them in a bulb frame which can be covered with lights during the dormant season.

D. ida-maia (*Brodiaea ida-maia, B. coccinea, Brevoortia ida-maia, B. coccinea*) The Fire Cracker Plant or Californian Fire Cracker. This is the most dramatic of the species but not one of the easiest to grow. Usually grows up to 25 or 30cm in height when in flower, but has been recorded as tall as 90cm. The leaves, usually three in number, are linear, basal, about 0·5–1cm wide and 30cm long, provided with a sharp keel on the underside and shallowly channelled above.

The flower stem is completely naked and carries an umbel of up to 12 pendulous flowers, each on a slender pedicel 1–5cm long. The flowers have a 2–3cm long bright crimson-red angular tube which gets wider towards the mouth, and six bright green reflexed lobes 0·5–0·9cm long. These eventually roll right back and become yellowish with age. The three sterile stamens are flattened and wide. forming a cream-coloured cup which protrudes beyond the mouth for about 0·3cm. The sterile anthers are also creamy and in turn project with the style beyond this cup. At fruiting time the pedicels become upright. Southern Oregon and northern California on grassy hills, in redwoods and deciduous forests, 300–1500m. Flowering May and June.

This plant was described by Alphonso Wood, in the genus *Brevoortia*, in 1867. He notes that it was 'first noticed by Mr Burke, the stage driver, in his daily route. He had given it the name Ida May in affection for his little daughter – a name quite appropriate, moreover, as on the Ides (i.e. the 15th) of May, the plant begins to flower.'

My own plants, grown from seed from Wayne Roderick, have flowered in a bulb frame where they are covered during the worst winter weather and in the summer. However they are no more successful than those planted out in a sunny border in Wessel Marais's garden in Hampton, Middlesex.

D. multiflorum (*Brodiaea capitata*) grows 20–80cm in height and has a congested umbel of narrow, pale to deep lilac-blue flowers with a whitish tube, each about 1·5–2cm long and carried more or less upright on pedicels varying from 0·3–1·5cm long. The tube is wide at the base, then narrows to a neck. The six lobes are about equal in length to the tube and are held out flat giving the individual flowers a spread of about 1cm. Oregon and California on grassy slopes and among oaks up to 1700m.

D. congesta is of rather similar appearance but has a tube 0·8–1cm long which is obviously six-angled. The flowers, although appearing to be produced in an umbel, are really in a very compact raceme. Washington State south through Oregon to California.

D. pulchellum The only species having six fertile stamens. This also has a densely-congested umbel like *D. multiflorum* but the individual flowers are rather more bell-shaped, with lobes 0·7–1cm long and a tube 0·5–0·8cm long which is not constricted. The umbel is surrounded by deep-purplish bracts and the flowers are blue-violet, rarely white, carried often on very short pedicels. The most widely-distributed species from Oregon to southern California and east to southwest Utah in grassy places up to 1800m.

D. venustum A striking plant 40–90cm in height with a loose umbel of pendulous flowers, rose-red in colour. The tube is cylindrical, 14–17mm long, slightly swollen at the base, and the segments about 0·8cm long. Rather rare in northwest California. It has been suggested in the past that this is a natural hybrid, and Dr Lee Lenz now considers it to be a cross between *D. ida-maia* and *D. multiflorum*, or possibly *D. congestum*. It is easily distinguished from *D. ida-*

maia in having the flowers wholly rose-coloured, not with the green segments of that species.

D. volubile The only species to have a twining flower stem, growing up to 120cm in height. The umbel is tight and carries up to 50 pinkish flowers with an inflated tube about 0·5cm long. The umbel is surrounded by pink bracts. California on the inner coastal ranges and in the Sierra foothills in chaparral, where it climbs through bushes. Since mentioning this plant in *Dwarf Bulbs*, I can report more success for it has increased very well in a bulb frame and is undamaged by frost, even when in leaf. The bulbs pull themselves down to a considerable depth and produce offsets quite freely. It should do well if planted at the edge of a Cistus or other small shrub where it will get evergreen protection and support for its twining stems.

Dierama Iridaceae

A South African genus of cormous plants with a widely fluctuating number of species, depending upon one's enthusiasm for 'splitting' or 'lumping'. The botanist N. E. Brown in the *Journal of the Royal Horticultural Society* 54:193 (1929) recognized 25 species. Several more have been described since then, bringing the total to about 30. At the other extreme, some people regard them all as forms of a few species only. The answer probably lies somewhere between the two, in the region of 15 or 20 but hardly any of these are in cultivation in Britain.

The main feature of *Dierama* is the long slender flower stem which arches over at the apex to cause the flowers to be pendulous, this graceful habit having given rise to the name 'Angel's Fishing Rod'. The bracts surrounding the flower are very papery and silver-white while the flowers themselves are bell-like with a short tube, in shades of pinkish-purple, deep wine or white. The erect wiry narrow leaves are more or less evergreen and this gives the clue that the corms must never be dried out too much in their dormant period. They all occur in the eastern part of South Africa or eastern tropical Africa and as a result make their main growth in Britain in summer, flowering in late summer. They are quite hardy but do best in mild areas with an ample supply of moisture during summer.

D. pulcherrimum The most commonly grown species here in Britain reaching about 120–150 cm in height. The flowers are about 3–5cm in length and are deep violet-purple in the wild but various varieties or hybrids have been raised which vary in the depth of colour. It occurs wild in grassy, seasonally moist places in the eastern Cape, Natal, Transvaal and Lesotho.

D. pendulum is a mountain plant from eastern tropical Africa from Ethiopia south to Rhodesia. It is very similar but has shorter flowers, less than 3cm in length, of a paler pinkish colour.

D. pumilum, as it occurs wild in Natal, is only about 60–80cm in height with white or yellowish flowers 1·3–1·5cm long. The name has also been given to short forms of *D. pulcherrimum*, which may be hybrids.

Dracunculus Araceae

D. vulgaris is a most impressive plant for a warm sunny place, where it increases well by division of the tubers. The thick false stem formed by the bases of the leaves is pale green, beautifully blotched and striped dark green, and reaches a height of 90cm. It is crowned by the striking leaf-blades which are deeply divided into five to seven lobes, the whole mature leaf-spread being about 30cm long and 30cm across at the base. In June from the centre of the fan of leaves emerges the inflorescence which consists of a green flask-shaped tube, expanded into a huge flat long-tapering blade of a deep rich matt maroon-purple. The spathe is about 30–45cm long and the erect darker shiny maroon spadix in the centre is about 30cm long. It has a disgusting smell rather like decaying meat and attracts flies. This handsome plant makes a fine show when planted in small clumps and should be surrounded by low-growing plants which accentuate its stature. It becomes completely dormant in winter and in cold districts should be covered with coarse peat or bracken for protection. A common Mediterranean plant, occurring in limestone country at low altitudes.

D. canariensis is not such a well-known plant in cultivation and is more tender, probably requiring greenhouse treatment. It has a smaller greenish spathe and a tapering yellow spadix. Canary Islands.

Endymion Liliaceae

See the genus *Hyacinthoides*, to which the English Bluebell belongs.

Fortunatia Liliaceae

This South American genus has now been included with the genus *Camassia* and the description of the species can be found there.

Fritillaria Liliaceae

Obviously many of the numerous species of fritillary are fairly short in stature and do not qualify for inclusion in this book, but the most spectacular species of all is the large and stately Crown Imperial. There are, however, several other tall ones which are well worth growing, and I have taken my minimum height limit as 'more than 30cm when in flower'.

The characteristics of *Fritillaria* species are pendulous flowers, shaped like a bell or cone, with a nectary at the base of each of its six perianth segments, a two-scaled bulb, or a more or less solid one producing many 'rice-grain' offsets, and a leafy stem with the leaves alternate, paired or whorled. It is unlikely that *Fritillaria* would be confused with any other genus although some of the North American species do resemble some species of *Lilium*. All of the species flower in spring, the taller species usually being the latest since they take longer to develop, but even the last of these is over by the end of May in southern England.

F. acmopetala About 30–40cm in height with scattered narrowly-linear grey leaves. The one to three large green pendent bells are 3–4cm long and 2–3cm wide with recurved tips to the segments. There is a variable amount of maroon on the inner three perianth segments and the pitted nectaries are deep green. Cyprus, southern Turkey, Syria, often in fields at low altitudes. Not a difficult plant to grow in reasonably mild areas such as the southern half of Britain. It should be given a well-drained sunny position.

F. arabica See *F. persica.*

F. askabadensis See *F. raddeana.*

F. camtschatcensis The Black Sarana. Bulb with masses of tiny offsets. Up to 40cm in height with glossy leaves arranged in dense whorls. The deep chocolate or blackish-purple bells, usually three or four but sometimes up to six, are produced in a compact raceme so that they almost appear to be in an umbel in extreme cases. Each flower is 2–3cm long and has ridges running along the inside surface of the segments. Occurs in eastern Asia, Japan and North America in the north-west states of Canada and USA. In cultivation this is a beautiful and easy plant if given a cool peaty spot where one would grow, for example, the autumn gentians, Hepatica, Trillium and Erythronium. Some forms 'run' underground by means of elongated rhizomes.

F. chitralensis See *F. imperialis.*

F. cirrhosa An extremely variable plant ranging from 15–100cm in height with scattered or whorled narrow leaves which usually have a tendril at the apex. These tendrils are used for support on neighbouring shrubs, but may be poorly developed if the plant is growing in the open. Flowers one to three, bell-shaped and rather flared at the mouth, up to 4cm long and 3cm wide, variable in colour from green with brown chequering to brown with green markings. Central and eastern Himalayas up to 500m on grassy hills and in scrub. *F. roylei* is very similar but has no tendrils on the leaves and comes from the western Himalayas.

F. coccinea See *F. recurva.*

F. eduardii See *F. imperialis.*

F. gentneri See *F. recurva.*

F. imperialis Crown Imperial. Stem up to 100cm in height, densely covered with whorled or alternate glossy leaves on the lower two-thirds, then leafless up to the flowers. The dense umbel is crowned with a further cluster of somewhat smaller leaves. Flowers several, pendulous, up to 6cm long and 5cm wide with a large white glistening nectary at the base of each segment inside. The most common form is brick-coloured but var. *lutea* and var. *chitralensis* have yellow flowers and var. *rubra* deep orange-red. *F. eduardii* from central southern Russia is orange with widely flaring bells and is probably only a form of *F. imperialis. F. raddeana* (*F. askabadensis*) inhabits eastern Iran and adjacent Russia and is a more slender, slightly smaller plant with pale greenish-yellow flowers.

F. imperialis itself occurs widely from south-east Turkey eastwards to the west Himalayas, usually on dry rocky slopes up to 2500m in altitude. It is a superb plant but is not easy to establish. It likes a warm sunny place with well-drained, preferably alkaline soil and once well-established should be left undisturbed for several years.

F. involucrata Up to 35cm in height with pairs of narrow grey leaves and a whorl of three overtopping the flowers. Flowers one to three wide bells up to 4cm long and 3cm wide, pale green with faint brown chequering. Maritime Alps of France and neighbouring Italy, in grassy places and open woods. Somewhat similar to *F. pontica* but the flowers have some chequering whereas those of *F. pontica* are completely without.

F. ionica See *F. pontica*.

F. lanceolata The most variable of the American species, ranging from small plants only 5cm in height with solitary large flowers, up to slender plants 40cm in height with a raceme of several smallish green or purple-brown pendulous flowers. The latter plants are usually the least attractive, for the flowers often have narrow non-overlapping segments. There is normally some amount of chequering to the flower. The leaves are whorled. Western Canada, south to California in gritty or rocky situations in and around pines and scrub up to 1800m altitude. *F. lanceolata*, like many of the American species, is not among the easiest of fritillaries to grow although it seems vigorous enough in the garden of Paul and Polly Furse in Kent. I have only succeeded with it in pots or bulb-frame beds, but it does not require too much of a baking in summer. It can be propagated by means of the numerous rice-grain bulblets which surround the flattish solid parent bulb.

F. libanotica See *F. persica*.

F. lusitanica (*F. hispanica*) A very variable plant up to 50cm in height with alternate linear or narrowly lanceolate leaves. Flowers up to 4cm long, solitary or, rarely, up to three, bell-shaped and slightly flared at the mouth, green or brownish, often with slight chequering and often with a pronounced green stripe along the centre of the segments. Spain and Portugal in open rocky places and light woodland. This is a good plant for growing in the open, at least in southern England, and it requires only a sunny spot in well-drained soil. It is especially vigorous on chalky soil.

F. meleagroides See *F. tenella*.

F. obliqua Grows up to 35cm tall with up to eight flowers in a raceme. The basal leaves are opposite and broader than the rest, which are alternate, lanceolate and somewhat twisted lengthways. All the leaves are greyish-green. Flowers up to four, conical, blackish-mahogany with a slight grey bloom, more or less pendent, 2–3cm long and 1·5–2cm wide. Rare in Greece, especially in Attica, in rocky places. It is not difficult in cultivation, given a well-drained sunny spot and an alkaline soil. *F. tuntasia* from the Cyclades is similar but slightly stronger-growing, with up to six flowers and many more leaves on the stem.

F. olivieri Up to 50cm high with three or four large bells of green with chocolate stripes. The leaves are rather shiny green, oblanceolate near the base of the stem and becoming narrower towards the apex. Each flower is about 4cm long and 2cm wide. It grows in moist meadows in western Iran and therefore does not require too much drying in summer. It is best grown in the open rather than a bulb frame.

F. oranensis This is extremely variable and the best forms for British gardens are probably those from high altitudes which are fairly dwarf. The species however grows up to 50cm in height in the vigorous low-altitude forms. The leaves of these taller plants are alternate, narrowly lanceolate, while the compact mountain forms have broad grey twisted leaves, the lowest of which are opposite. The flowers are solitary, or rarely two per stem, bell-shaped, chequered brown with a green stripe along the centre of the segments. The size varies a lot, but normally the bells are 3–4cm long. Algeria, Morocco and Tunisia in scrub and cedar forests up to 3000m. Not very hardy, so should be grown in a bulb frame or alpine house.

F. pallidiflora A beautiful species and one of the best for growing out of doors for it is very hardy and sets seed freely. Stem up to 50cm in height with opposite or alternate broad grey leaves. The one to four very square pale yellow bells are about 4cm long and 3cm wide and are usually spotted with red inside. Russia, in the Tien Shan and Ala Tau mountains up to 3000m. I find this one of the most accommodating of all fritillaries for it seems to grow in almost any reasonably good soil and seedlings do not take long to reach flowering size.

F. persica (*F. libanotica*, *F. arabica*) Very distinct in the genus in having a long raceme of flowers with no leaf-like bracts subtending their pedicels. Stem up to 100cm in height with many lanceolate grey leaves packed on to the lower half. Inflorescence leafless, with up to 30 conical pendulous flowers 1–2cm long. They vary in colour from deep plum to straw yellow, but the former forms are by far the most attractive. A particularly vigorous blackish-plum-coloured form grows in southern Turkey and has been given the cultivar name of 'Adiyaman' after the town of the same name. *F. persica* occurs over a wide area from Cyprus and southern Turkey east to central Iran. It grows in fields or on stony hills up to 2500m. The only problem in cultivation in Britain is if there is a heavy frost after the young shoots have emerged when damage is likely to occur. A sunny sheltered spot is therefore necessary. The warm dry spring of 1976 suited it very well in my Surrey garden and it set a large quantity of seeds.

F. pontica One of the easiest species to grow in most parts of Britain and North America since it is very hardy and prefers a cool position. Up to 45cm in height with lowest leaves opposite, the upper alternate, lanceolate near the base and nearly linear higher up. The top three are produced in a whorl overtopping the flowers. Flowers one to three large bells up to 4·5cm long, usually a delicate apple-green colour with a slight suffusion of brown at the tips and margins of the segments. The nectaries within are very obvious since they are very dark green. Occurs in Macedonia and Albania east to southern Bulgaria and the Pontic mountains of Turkey, usually in heavy clay soils in the shade of pines or deciduous woods up to 1000m altitude. *F. graeca* var. *thessala* (*F. ionica*) from Corfu and north-west Greece is very similar but has slightly chequered flowers.

F. raddeana See *F. imperialis*.

F. recurva Probably the most dramatic of the fritillaries since it has red flowers unlike any other. Grows to 40cm in height with whorls of narrow leaves, or alternate ones in young or weak plants. Flowers one to six up to 3cm long, narrowly bell-shaped with recurved tips to the segments, bright red or orange with faint chequering. Var. *coccinea* is a mixture of red and yellow mottling and the segments are not reflexed. *F. gentneri* may only be a variant of *F. recurva*; it too has reddish flowers, although with a purplish tinge, and segments which do not reflex. *F. recurva* grows wild in Oregon and California up to 2200m altitude in humus-rich soils near and under pines. It is not a very easy species in cultivation although it grows well in the Suffolk garden of Sir Cedric Morris. The best chance of success seems to be to plant it out in a bulb frame and leave it undisturbed. Propagation is no problem, for the flattish bulbs produce many offsets – the difficulty lies in growing these on to flowering size.

F. roylei See *F. cirrhosa*.

F. ruthenica See *F. tenella*.

F. sewerzovii Recognized by some botanists as a separate genus, *Korolkowia*. This grows up to 45cm in height and has broad elliptic or lanceolate alternate leaves with up to 15 flowers in each of the upper leaf axils. Each is narrowly bell-shaped and widely flared at the mouth, about 2–3cm long and green or brownish with a grey bloom. Russia, in the Tien Shan and Pamir mountains up to 2000m. Not a difficult plant to grow in a bulb frame or alpine house but does not seem to do very well out of doors in Britain. It is hardy but seems to need protection from wet and cold weather in winter.

F. stribrnyi A rare species in cultivation, growing to about 40cm in height but sometimes up to twice as high. Leaves alternate, very narrow with the upper three in a whorl. Flowers one to three narrow bells 2–3cm long, 1–5cm wide, green with a purplish suffusion at the edges and tips of the segments, covered with a greyish bloom. European Turkey and southern Bulgaria in scrub and grassy places. My bulbs were given to me by Professor Baytop of Istanbul and I have not yet tried them in the open ground. It does not seem to be a difficult species in the bulb frame and flowered the first year after I received them.

F. tenella Up to 50cm in height with many very narrow leaves varying from alternate to paired or whorled. Flowers one to three pendulous bells up to 3cm long and 2cm wide, deep brownish-purple and checked. Italy, France and south-east Europe in grassy places or woods. *F. ruthenica* from south-east Russia is very similar but has tendril-like tips to the upper leaves and one to five deep blackish-brown flowers about 2·5cm long. *F. meleagroides*, which usually has solitary flowers and occurs in southern Russia and southern Bulgaria, is very close to this but all the leaves are alternate, normally without tendrils.

F. tenella is an accommodating species, perfectly easy in the open border in southern England. It does not require a sun-baked position.

F. thunbergii See *F. verticillata*.

F. tuntasia See *F. obliqua*.

F. verticillata Stems to 60cm in height with whorls of lanceolate leaves, the upper ones tendril-like. Flowers up to six in the axils of the upper leaves, about 2·5cm long, conical, cream with green veining. Russia, eastern China and Japan. An easy plant to grow outside in Britain and North America but it often splits up continually into small bulbs which will not flower. Don Elick has sent me a form which he found in Japan, apparently very free flowering, but it is too early yet to say if it will retain this desirable feature in cultivation here. *F. thunbergii* is probably only a form of *F. verticillata* for it is scarcely distinguishable.

Galtonia Liliaceae

A small genus of striking South African plants of which one, the white flowered *G. candicans*, is quite well-known and easily obtainable. The other two species have greenish flowers and are not grown to any extent although they have a subtle charm. In the northern hemisphere they all flower in mid to late summer and are hardy in mild areas, especially if the bulbs can be given some protection with bracken or granular peat in the winter. *G. princeps* is probably the most tender and I have grown this in a cool greenhouse border although it does well in a sheltered spot against a sunny wall in the garden of Wessel Marais. As a precaution the bulbs of all the species can be lifted in autumn for storage in a frost-free place and planted out in spring. Seed is produced freely and this can be grown on quite rapidly to flowering-sized bulbs. In fruit the pedicels become erect.

G. candicans grows up to 120cm in height in flower with long, slightly greyish-green leaves about 5cm wide, narrowing gradually to the apex. Inflorescence a loose raceme of up to 30 flowers. Flowers pendulous, carried on pedicels up to 6cm long, about 3cm long, rather bell-shaped, white; the perianth lobes are longer than the tube. Orange Free State, Natal and Lesotho, from 1500–2100m on rocky ledges and sandy soils. This grows well on acid sandy soils such as at Wisley and makes a good clump in a border or among shrubs for a late summer display.

G. princeps is generally a little smaller than *G. candicans* but the leaves are similar in shape. Flowers rather trumpet-shaped, usually greenish-cream, less than 3cm in length with the lobes about equal to the tube. Natal and Transkei, at lower altitudes on the edges of forest and bush land. A surprising method of propagation was found by Miss P. Halliday when making the illustration of this species. I had cut an entire plant at ground level, and after drawing it she had left it in a vase for several weeks. The cut surfaces of the leaves had produced many small bulbs in the same way that the scales of Lilies will if detached.

11 *Galtonia princeps*

G. viridiflora A rather different looking species with leaves up to 10cm broad, narrowing abruptly to the apex which then is furnished with a short blunt tip. The flowers are rather trumpet-shaped, usually pale green, about 2–5cm long with the lobes longer than the tube. Distribution similar to *G. candicans*.

Gelasine Iridaceae

A small South American genus of blue-flowered bulbous plants only one of which has been grown in Britain to any extent. Two or three other species have been described but the lack of any living or dried material makes it impossible for me to comment upon them at present.

G. azurea A strong plant up to 90cm in height with a loose-scaled reddish bulb, four basal bluish-green pleated leaves and usually one similar stem leaf. The flowering stem consists of one to several long branches arising from the axils of small leaf-like bracts with terminal inflorescences of tightly folded bracts enclosing many flowers. Flowers flattish with six equal segments produced in long succession, each opening for one morning only, 4–5cm in diameter, deep blue but whitish towards the base and speckled with blue. The style and anthers are deep purple-blue with white pollen and the filaments join to form a tube around the style which is trilobed at the apex. The capsule is very fat, about 1·5cm long when mature and contains very many seeds. Southern Brazil and Uruguay in grassy places below 1000m. This has done well with me planted in a cool greenhouse border where it is very vigorous and produces a great quantity of seed. The flowers are short-lived but many are produced for at least a month and they are of such an intense colour that it is a favourite of mine. It grows in the summer months here and flowers in July so that it could be planted out in spring in a warm spot and lifted for the winter.

G. caerulea looks to be rather similar but has fewer leaves and produces long cylindrical seed capsules about 5cm long and 1cm wide.

Gladiolus Iridaceae

A familiar and popular genus of probably 150 species, now including the genus *Acidanthera*. Of these, just over 100 are from southern Africa, the rest tropical African with a few in Europe and western Asia. The whole genus can be roughly divided into two groups, summer rainfall and winter rainfall. These terms apply just the same when we cultivate them in Britain or North America: those from the south-west Cape, Europe, north Africa and Asia occur in winter rainfall regions and those from the eastern Cape are in a summer rainfall area. The tropical African species behave in the same way as the latter so can be treated similarly, although the terms summer and winter do not really apply to these tropical countries. In cultivation, the winter rainfall species are started into growth in autumn and they flower the following spring, while the summer rainfall species are kept dry during the winter and are started into growth in late spring. Obviously the latter species are more satisfactory since the corms can be stored during the worst weather and planted out in spring. Some of the summer rainfall ones are hardy in Britain, coming from the high mountain ranges such as the Drakensberg of Lesotho and Natal, in the eastern half of southern Africa. It is mainly the summer rainfall species which have been used in hybridization to produce the large flowered showy gladioli of today. Most of the species from winter rainfall regions are tender in Britain and need to be grown in a frost-free greenhouse in all but very mild areas. Those from Europe and Asia are much hardier, of course, and can mostly be grown outside if given a sunny well-drained position.

The *Gladiolus* flower looks at first to be rather complicated, but in fact has all the features of the Iridaceae without any very highly developed floral parts such as those of some genera such as *Iris*. The flowers are produced in a spike which is either one-sided (secund) – that is with the flowers facing all in one direction – or two-sided (distichous), with the flowers facing alternately in opposite directions. Each flower is normally irregular in shape and held horizontally but some species are nearly symmetrical and upright. The six segments are joined into a distinct tube, sometimes a very long one, up to 15cm, and the tube is very often curved. Some species have six equal segments and a regular flower but the most usual gladiolus flower is a rather irregularly shaped one, with the segments of differing shapes and sizes. The upper one is often hooded over to form a protective covering for the stamens and style which arch up to lie beneath it. The lower three segments often have coloured markings on them, presumably to advertise to pollinating insects.

Northern hemisphere species The species of Gladiolus from Europe and western Asia are on the whole less showy than the tropical or South African ones but have the obvious advantage that they are hardy and make their growth during the spring and early summer months. Several of them, however, require plenty of sun and a dryish warm soil during their dormant period in late summer and may require bulb-bed treatment. They flower in late spring and early summer.

G. atroviolaceus (*C. aleppicus*) Many collections of this have been introduced during the last ten years but it still remains an uncommon plant in cultivation. 30–50cm in height with three narrow leaves. Spike one-sided, fairly dense with about five to ten very dark violet flowers 4–4·5cm long. The two lower lateral segments are longer than the rest. This is a very common plant in Turkey, Iran and Iraq in fields and can be very impressive when seen in great quantity, appearing almost black in the distance. The most successful method of cultivation has been in a bulb frame, but sunny warm beds should be satisfactory, especially on alkaline soils. *G. kotschyanus* is rather similar in colour and general appearance but the leaves do not have parallel veins for their entire length as in *G. atroviolaceus*. It inhabits wet meadows in Iran, Iraq and eastern Turkey and should not require bulb-frame treatment.

G. byzantinus A useful hardy plant which increases well in sunny borders, especially on chalk. Stems 50–100cm high with a fan of three to five rather broad leaves. Spike often branched, rather lax and more or less two-sided with up to 20 flowers. Each flower 6–7cm long, rich purple-red with a white stripe along the centre of the lower segment. Occurs wild in southern Spain, Sicily and north Africa. The form which is in cultivation is very vigorous. A white form, 'Albus', is a rather rare and beautiful variation.

G. communis This is very similar to *G. byzantinus* but usually has pinkish flowers with the lowest segment often marked with dark and light central stripes. It is widespread throughout southern Europe.

G. halophilus A slender species 20–40cm in height with leaves only 2–3mm wide. The purple to rose flowers are 3–3·5cm long and are produced in a lax one-sided spike. The segments are unequal, with the upper one and the lower two laterals longer than the lower one and the upper two laterals. Iran, Iraq and south-east Turkey on open hillsides to 2200m.

G. illyricus The only Gladiolus to occur naturally in England where it is very rare and should never be picked. A smallish species, 30–50cm in height with about five to ten reddish-purple flowers in a lax two-sided spike which is rarely branched. The lower segment has darker purplish and white markings. The two upper lateral are slightly shorter than the rest. North Africa and southern Europe northwards to southern England in fields and stony places to 1500m.

G. imbricatus This usually has only one broad basal leaf and one or two narrower stem leaves and reaches 30–80cm. The inflorescence is sometimes branched, distinctly one-sided and rather dense with two to ten flowers. The colour is violet-to-reddish-purple and the segments are more or less equal in length. Central and eastern Europe, Turkey in wet meadows and scrubland.

G. italicus (*G. segetum*) Perhaps the best-known of all the northern hemisphere species since it is a common plant in fields throughout the Mediterranean region. 50–100cm in height with a fan of four to five leaves, the lowest rather broad and the upper narrower but the tips all reaching to about the same level. Flowers up to 15, rather laxly arranged in a more or less two-sided spike, reddish-lilac and about 4–5cm long. The upper segment and the lower three are all about equal in length and longer than the remaining two. The only way in which I have satisfactorily grown this in England is in a bulb frame, but it should succeed in warm well-drained spots, especially on chalky soils. North Africa, southern Europe, the Canaries and Asia Minor east to USSR and Afghanistan.

G. palustris 25–50cm in height with two basal leaves and one stem leaf. The distinctly one-sided loose unbranched spike has only two to six flowers of a reddish-purple. Usually inhabits wet meadows, in central Europe.

G. persicus Not a well-known species. Leaves three, exceeding the flower spike, very narrow, usually between 1·5 and 3·5mm wide. The two-sided spike has dark violet-purple flowers about 3–3·5cm long with the upper middle segment much longer and broader than the others; the three lower segments are longer than the two upper lateral ones. Leaves, stems and bracts are all finely pubescent. Open hillsides in Iran.

G. triphyllus This is a small species only 10–40cm in height with leaves only 2–8mm wide and a short spike with up to six flowers, although it often has only one or two. It is salmon pink with purple or whitish markings on the lower segments; the flower is only 2–3·5cm long, with the upper middle and lower three segments longer than the two upper lateral ones. It occurs in fields, maquis and pinewoods from sea level to 1350m on Cyprus.

Eastern Cape and tropical African species These are grouped together, since in Britain they tend to behave as summer-growing plants with a dormant period in winter. Thus they differ in their treatment from the south-west Cape species which come from winter-rainfall areas and in Britain continue to make their growth through the winter months, flowering in early spring and becoming dormant for the summer. Obviously the species from the tropics are rather tender, although many of the species are mountain plants and may be more hardy than one would expect. The eastern Cape species are much more reliable out of doors and a few can be left out for the winter, although as a generalization all the species are best lifted for the winter and stored in a frost-free shed or garage. Our large-flowered hybrid Gladiolus are mostly derived from eastern Cape species and their treatment in gardens is basically the one which should be adopted for the wild species from these summer rainfall areas. In cold districts they should not be planted out before the end of April and must be given a warm well-drained position. Alternatively they can be planted out in a greenhouse border or a frame which can be covered over in winter with lights to keep out the frost.

G. callianthus A new name for a well-known plant, previously named *Acidanthera bicolor*. This graceful plant is one of the most attractive of the Gladiolus species with its long curving slender perianth tube and sweetly scented flowers. Grows up to 110cm in height with a few narrowly lanceolate leaves up to 2cm wide. Flowers up to ten, about 4–5cm in diameter with more or less equal perianth segments, pure white with a prominent purple blotch near the centre. The perianth tube is up to 12cm long. *G. callianthus* is an easy plant to grow but is not hardy in most parts of Britain. Near the Sussex coast it persisted and flowered for many years in the chalky soil in a hot sunny spot but even in Surrey I do not find it winter-hardy. The corms should be planted in a warm sheltered position in early May and lifted in autumn before any serious frosts occur. I normally pot up the corms in March or April and keep them in a greenhouse until the frosts are over, then plant them out. *G. callianthus* occurs wild in the eastern half of Africa from Ethiopia to Malawi on the higher mountains on damp cliffs up to 2000m. In Britain it flowers in September or October. Several selections have been made differing only slightly from each other in the time of flowering and the stiffness of the growth. They are offered by nurseries as *Acidanthera bicolor* (*G. callianthus*), *A. murielae* (*G. callianthus* 'Murielae') and *A. tubergenii* 'Zwanenburg' (*G. callianthus* 'Zwanenburg').

G. cardinalis See *G. sempervirens*.

G. cruentus See *G. sempervirens*.

G. natalensis (*G. psittacinus, G. quartinianus*). A robust species up to 1–1·5m in height. The corm produces many offsets, sometimes at the end of long runners. Leaves five to ten, up to 60cm long and 3cm broad. Spike one-sided with up to 25 flowers, but only a few opening at a time. Flowers 5–8cm across with a curved funnel-shaped tube 2–5cm long; upper three segments hooded, the lower three smaller and rather reflexed. It is very variable in colour from plain red, orange or yellow to variously spotted and tinged with green or brown, and often with a paler zone on the lower segments. It inhabits a variety of situations usually in grassland from sea level to high mountain slopes. In the Kenya uplands I have seen the spectacular orange speckled form dotted amongst the dry brown grass at over 2000m. Widespread in Africa from Ethiopia south to the eastern Cape; also in western Arabia. It flowers at different times of year in the wild, depending upon the rainy season; mid to late summer in Britain. *G. primulinus* is a charm-

Allium rosenbachianum, a very showy 'onion' which requires a sunny well-drained spot

Arisaema candidissimum is by far the best species of Arisaema in British gardens

Camassia quamash (esculenta), a fine summer bulb for planting in grass

Dierama pendula, a graceful African plant for a warm position

12 *Gladiolus illyricus*
13 *Gladiolus papilio (purpureo-auratus)*
14 *Gladiolus saundersiae*

15 *Gladiolus tristis* var. *concolor*
16 *Gladiolus segetum*
17 *Gladiolus imbricatus*

ing, clear primrose-yellow form of this species from east and south tropical Africa. *G. garnieri* from Madagascar is similar in size and general appearance to *G. natalensis* but has all the segments recurved at their tips, including the upper one, which is not hooded as much as in that species. The colour is a clear orange-pink with a yellow centre. My plants originated from Maurice Boussard of Verdun, to whom I am indebted for many rare Iridaceae. *G. melleri* is like a slender smaller-flowered version of *G. natalensis* in deep salmon, cream and yellow forms. The flowering stem is usually nearly leafless, the leaves appearing on a separate shoot. It occurs on the uplands of east and south tropical Africa in damp grassy places.

G. papilio (*G. purpureo-auratus*) One of the parents of the Butterfly hybrids. A strongly stoloniferous plant up to 100cm in height with four to five basal leaves 0·5–2cm wide. Spike with up to ten flowers, but usually far less in cultivation, more or less one-sided and drooping over rather than erect. Flowers about 5–6cm long, strongly hooded, often with the segments not at all flared outwards so that the flowers are a curved bell-shape, because of the curved tube. The colour is very variable from yellow to green, often suffused with purple, especially on the lower three segments. Throughout the eastern part of southern Africa in damp meadows up to 2000m. This is not a showy species but nevertheless has a charm which many people enjoy since it has the same colour mixtures as many species of Fritillaria. The form which I have grown for a long time has flowers of a green and purple mixture. It is very vigorous and completely hardy, very rapidly producing large patches because of its stolon-forming habit, and in fact in some small terraced beds it became invasive. Open shrub borders would seem to be a more appropriate place where it has room to spread freely without swamping small plants.

G. psittacinus See *G. natalensis*.

G. quartinianus See *G. natalensis*.

G. saundersiae 40–90cm in height with five or six rather stiffly erect basal leaves 0·5–2·5cm wide. Spike one-sided with up to ten flowers. Flowers large, bright red with the basal half of the three lower segments white; the upper segment is rather hooded over and reflexed at the tip while the remaining five are flared outwards. Drakensberg Mountains of Lesotho and Natal and adjacent parts of the eastern Cape in grassy and rocky places, almost reaching 3000m. Rather similar to *G. sempervirens* but has the large white areas on the lower segments and a curved perianth tube. I have grown and flowered this showy species for several years out of doors in Surrey, both against a south-west wall and a south-facing fence, where it flowered in late summer. The corms were left in all year without extra protection in winter but the rate of increase has been very slow.

G. sempervirens (*G. splendens* Baker) An evergreen species reaching 50–100cm in height, forming tufts because of the persistent dead leaves. Corm strongly stoloniferous; basal leaves rather tough and rigid, about 30cm long; stem leaves much shorter. The one-sided spike has 2–10 large, bright red flowers; perianth tube nearly straight; the upper segment is held over the stamens and the other five are flared outwards. The lower three have a small white central spear-shaped mark. Eastern Cape, but near the border between the summer and winter rainfall areas and therefore scarcely dormant. It grows in damp places on ledges and in forests up to 1700m. My own plants have been grown in a sandy bed in a cool greenhouse where they increase rapidly by stolons. The species is probably hardy in mild areas. Flowers in late summer in the northern hemisphere. *G. cardinalis* is rather similar but occurs in the southern Cape near streams and on wet ledges. The corm is not stoloniferous and it is a deciduous plant with lighter red flowers and a more hooded upper segment. The lower segments have larger white markings. The flower spike is pendulous, hanging over the cliffs which the plant inhabits. *G. cruentus* is another of the red-flowered eastern species from the mountains of Natal and Lesotho and is similar to *G. sempervirens*, with an erect inflorescence, not pendulous as in *G. cardinalis*. It is, however, a deciduous species, occurring on severe cliff faces in the Drakensberg. It is one of the parents of the modern hybrid gladiolus.

G. splendens See *G. sempervirens*.

G. ukambanensis (*Acidanthera laxiflora*) A close relative of *G. callianthus* (*A. bicolor*) differing mainly in having creamy or yellowish-coloured flowers with a poorly defined purplish blotch in the centre, or completely white. It is a smaller plant but if anything more graceful with very slender growth. The flower is regular, of six equal segments, and has a tube up to 10cm long. Occurs in eastern Africa from Ethiopia south to Tanzania in damp grassy places. This species is, like its larger relative, not hardy in Britain but can be successfully grown in large pots or tubs on the patio where its sweetly scented white flowers are attractive on warm summer evenings. If planted out in the open ground the corms must be lifted in autumn and stored in a frost-free place.

South-west Cape species The south-west Cape species of Gladiolus (and for that matter most 'bulbs' from that area) are winter-growing plants, normally flowering at the end of the season between July and November. In Britain they continue to behave in this way, growing through our winter and flowering in January to April. This, of course, presents a problem since they are not hardy and are normally growing in a region of reasonably high light intensity. We must therefore grow them in a cool greenhouse and give them as much light and air as possible. It is best to either plant them out into beds in the greenhouse or grow them in pots, but in the latter case re-potting annually, or at least every two years, is necessary. The corms are started into growth in August–September by watering and are then kept growing until after flowering when most of them are dried off for the summer. A few which occur in damp places, or in the southern Cape in the transition area between winter and summer rainfall areas, do not require too much baking in summer. Any special notes about cultivation such as this will be dealt with under the species concerned.

G. blandus See *G. carneus*.

G. carmineus A beautiful species which grows successfully in my cool green-house but it must be treated slightly differently from the south-west Cape species. It flowers in late summer and needs to be kept growing much longer, still having green leaves when the others are completely dormant. A sturdy species not more than 35cm in height with one or two long narrow greyish leaves produced after flowering, often trailing on the ground as they are weak and not self-supporting. Flowers two to five produced in a compact one-sided spike, deep pink or a strong carmine with a white central marking on each of the lower segments. The segments are roughly equal in size and shape giving an almost regular flower about 4–6cm across. Southern Cape, near the sea on damp cliffs. This could perhaps be placed with the summer rainfall species here as it falls half-way in its cultivation needs. It should be started into growth in late summer and kept growing until early summer the following year.

G. carneus (*G. blandus*) A delightful species which has been cultivated in Britain at least since the 18th century, perhaps one of the very first to be introduced, and in 1822 William Herbert wrote that he had hybrids between *G. carneus* and various other species. It is an extremely variable species, 20–100cm in height with about five to ten wide funnel-shaped flowers each 5–8cm long. The colour varies from white to pink and purple, usually with paler or darker well-defined markings on the lower three segments and with or without deeper coloured blotches in the throat. South-west Cape, up to 1200m in a variety of habitats from sandy places to mountain slopes. Flowering February–March in Britain, September–December in the wild. This is an easy species in cultivation in Britain and I have grown it successfully in pots or planted out in a cool green-house border. In mild areas it can be grown out of doors. The white form is sometimes offered by nurseries.

G. grandis See *G. tristis*.

G. liliaceus See *G. tristis*.

G. orchidiflorus A particular favourite of mine, since it has smallish scented flowers in a mixture of green and purple, although it does vary a lot in colour. Grows up to 50cm in height with up to eight very narrow leaves. Flowers five to 15 in a more or less one-sided spike, each 3–5cm long and 2–3cm wide, very irregular in shape. The upper segment is narrow and arched right over the top of the flower, hooding the stamens and style. The two segments on either side of this, and the lowest one, are broader and have a purple line along the centre. The two lower lateral segments are narrower and spoon-shaped with a purple blotch in the centre, or have a purplish suffusion on a yellowish or greenish background. South-west Cape, Namaqualand and Orange Free State, occurring in sandy places. I have grown this for some years from corms given to me by Georges Delpierre and Johan Loubser and it has proved to be one of the easier of the winter-growing species. It has been most successful in deep pots in a cool greenhouse, watered from September onwards until flowering time in February. Water is gradually reduced and then withheld altogether for the summer. It is a very variable species and the overall colour of the flowers can be green, a rather pale silvery-purple or a muddy yellow. Propagation is very easy since it produces many cormlets around the parent.

G. tristis A well-known species and a particularly attractive one, for its pale yellow or creamy-white flowers are sweetly scented in the evenings. Variable in height from 50–150cm, with very narrow leaves, cross-shaped in section. Flowers usually ten, sometimes up to 20 in a one-sided spike, each with a tube 4–8cm long and a spread of 3–5cm. The lower five segments are nearly equal, with pointed tips and the upper one rather broader. South-west Cape in sandy damp places up to 1800m altitude. There are three varieties of this in the wild, var. *tristis* with flowers striped and stippled green or brownish on a creamy background, var. *concolor* with plain pale yellow or cream flowers and var. *aestivalis* with many more flowers, up to 20 in number, produced rather late in the season. The flowering period of var. *tristis* in cultivation in Britain is January to May. I have not tried to grow var. *aestivalis*. *G. tristis* is sometimes grown out of doors in south-west England where it will stay year after year without damage in winter. In the south-east it survives most winters but is not reliably hardy. The race of small-flowered *Gladiolus* known as *G. colvillei* and *G. nanus* were derived from a cross between *G. tristis* and *G. cardinalis*. There are various named cultivars such as 'The Bride' (white), 'Amanda Mahy' (rich salmon), 'Peach Blossom' (rose blotched with cream) and 'Spitfire' (brilliant vermilion). The corms of these should be planted in autumn in a warm sunny border and left undisturbed. If a very severe winter is expected, then bracken should be placed over the bed. *G. liliaceus* (*G. grandis*) is rather similar to *G. tristis* but has only one to four, brown to deep-red, scented flowers with long tapering recurved tips to the segments. The colour of the flowers is said to become brighter in the evenings, although I have not seen this in cultivated plants. It is rather uncommon in the south-west Cape.

G. undulatus A graceful species but not flowering very freely in cultivation, nor in the wild either, according to Delpierre and Du Plessis. Usually 30–70cm in height, with a two-sided spike of up to 15 flowers, each 8–10cm long and 4–6cm diameter, with a long funnel-shaped tube and roughly equal segments with elegant long-pointed tips. The colour is extremely variable from white to greenish and pink, often with spear-shaped purple markings on the lower three segments. The segments are often rather wavy, this presumably having suggested the epithet 'undulatus'. South-west Cape in damp places on hill slopes. *G. undulatus* is easy to grow and produces cormlets for propagation purposes but in my cool greenhouse it does not flower very often. It is nearly hardy in the south-east of England and will naturalize in very mild areas.

Gloriosa Liliaceae

This beautiful genus of mainly tropical and subtropical plants from Africa and India has many variants which have been described as species at one time or another, resulting in about 30 names. However, one of my colleagues at Kew, Dr D. V. Field, regards them all as forms of one species, *G. superba*. In the Royal Horticultural Society's publication *Lilies and other Liliaceae* (1973), he explains how difficult, or even impossible, it is to distinguish between the various forms, since intermediates occur.

Gloriosa produces a leafy stem from a tuberous rootstock, the tubers being rather finger-like and dividing up as they grow, so that propagation is merely a matter of separating them when re-potting or re-planting. The large flowers are produced in the axils of the leaves. Each flower is nodding, but the petals reflex sharply, leaving the stamens and style protruding very prominently. The style has the curious feature of bending sharply at right angles to the axis of the flower. The perianth segments, which are usually rather narrow and do not overlap, are often crisped or undulate at the edges. The colour varies from deep red to deep yellow or bicoloured with a yellow margin to red segments. There are tall forms up to 2·5m in height, with tendrils on the ends of the leaves, which climb on shrubs; tall forms without tendrils; dwarf forms with and without tendrils; and narrow and broad-leaved forms. Some of the various names to be found in catalogues and other books are:

G. abyssinica A form with leaf tendrils, of medium height, usually with yellow flowers.

G. carsonii A tall form with poorly developed leaf tendrils and purplish flowers edged with yellow on the segments.

G. lutea A medium height form with leaf tendrils and soft-yellow flowers with wavy segments.

G. minor A really dwarf form from the semi-deserts of northern Kenya. It has very narrow leaves densely packed on the 30cm stems and often one·terminal flower, although I have seen it with more. The colour is a dull tomato red.

G. rothschildiana A very large-flowered, tall, climbing or sprawling form with leaf tendrils. The flowers are bright red with yellow at the base of the segments which are very undulate at their margins. Var. *citrina* is a yellow, purple-stained variant of this.

G. simplex Dr D. V. Field regards this as an uncertain name, to be disposed of.

G. superba A very widespread form in Africa and India, and the best known. This has deep orange-red or yellow flowers with non-wavy margins to the very narrow perianth segments. It is a tall climbing one with leaf tendrils.

G. virescens This is like *G. superba* but has undulating segments about 2cm wide, about twice the width of those of *G. superba*.

Although this is some sort of guide to the names, it must be remembered that Gloriosas are very variable and intermediate forms can occur. Additionally, it is possible for a form with no leaf tendrils to produce them if it has the possibility of climbing. Even with the dwarf *G. minor*, which is self-supporting normally, I have seen tendrils produced on plants growing in a small bush. Dr Field recommends that to distinguish between all these various forms for garden purposes a system of cultivar names should be used.

Hippeastrum Amaryllidaceae

Popularly but incorrectly known as 'Amaryllis'. This is a large genus of about 65 species of showy bulbs. They occur wild from the West Indies and Mexico southwards to Argentina and are not hardy in Britain, although a few of the higher altitude species from temperate South America may survive outside in sheltered positions in the south. The umbel of flowers is carried on a robust leafless stem, which is lateral to the basal fan of strap-shaped or lanceolate leaves. The six perianth segments are often unequal giving the flower a rather irregular appearance, and the stamens all curve downwards to the lower side of the flower and are of differing lengths. All Hippeastrums have a perianth tube but it varies a great deal from species to species; in some as little as 1cm, whereas in others the most attractive feature is the very long slender tube. Since the early nineteenth century several of the species have been used in hybridization and most of the gaudy 'Amaryllis' which are sold today as winter-flowering pot plants are of obscure parentage.

H. advenum This reaches about 30cm in height when in flower and produces an umbel of horizontal funnel-shaped 3–4·5cm long flowers which are red with a yellowish median line along each of the rather narrow segments. The leaves appear at the end of the flowering period, which is August or September in Britain. It occurs wild in Chile. *H. advenum* is one of the hardiest species and can be grown out of doors in the south-west of Britain. Normally, however, it is best grown as a cool greenhouse plant.

H. pratense This species is hardy in very mild areas but even in Surrey it succumbs to light frosts so it is best regarded as a plant for the greenhouse. It grows to about 30cm in height and has a few bright red funnel-shaped flowers, produced in early summer together with the leaves. They are larger than those of *H. advenum*. It is also a native of Chile.

Hyacinthoides Liliaceae

The name of our common English Bluebell has, we hope, at last become stable and will remain *H. non-scripta*. The genus contains only three or four species, differing from *Scilla* in having two bracts subtending each flower and a curious non-scaly bulb which is replaced completely by a new one each year. Apart from the two well-known robust species described below there is the easily grown *H. italica* from south-west Europe, which has a dense conical inflorescence and flattish deep blue-violet flowers. This is usually about 10–20cm in height. *H. vicentina* from southern Portugal differs from this in having a more lax inflorescence and yellow stamens, instead of bluish ones as in *H. italica*. *H. reverchonii* (*Scilla reverchonii*) from south-east Spain is similar to *H. italica* but the lax raceme has flowers which are more campanulate than flat.

H. hispanica Spanish Bluebell. A robust plant forming large very floriferous clumps and very useful for a semi-wild garden. Grows up to 40cm with strap-shaped leaves usually a little shorter than the racemes. Usually it produces about ten to 15 flowers in a lax raceme, widely bell-shaped, blue, pink or white. The anthers are bluish. It occurs wild in Spain and Portugal and flowers in May in Britain. There are several named cultivars differing in flower colour.

H. non-scripta English Bluebell (*Scilla non-scripta, Endymion nutans*) Almost too well-known to need a description and some people will object to its being included here, for it can be an awful weed in some gardens. It grows to 35cm in height with a rather one-sided lax raceme of blue, pink or white long bell-shaped flowers. The raceme bends over at the apex, a point of difference between it and *H. hispanica*, and in addition the anthers are creamy-white. The segments do not spread quite as much as those of *H. hispanica*, giving a more tubular-shaped flower. Occurs wild in western Europe, mainly in woodlands, where it flowers in April. In gardens it will hybridize with *H. hispanica* producing a confusing range of intermediates. It is best grown in semi-wild situations where it can be left to naturalize, since it is far too vigorous for inclusion in a rock garden or in peat beds, where it can take over.

Hyacinthus Liliaceae

A very small genus of only three or four species, the remainder having been removed to other related genera, such as *Bellevalia, Brimeura, Pseudomuscari* and *Hyacinthella*. Most of the species in this group are, however, fairly dwarf plants and will not be dealt with here. *Hyacinthus* species have true bulbs, a cluster of broadly linear or lanceolate basal leaves and a raceme of flowers. These are long-tubed, the stamens being hidden well down inside the tube. The six perianth segments often recurve somewhat.

H. orientalis The species which has given rise to the great range of garden varieties now available, purely through selection as no other species has been involved. The wild species can reach up to 30–40cm in height with a lax raceme of two to 15 very fragrant mid-blue or white flowers, each about 0·5–2cm long with a long tube and reflexing lobes. Wild in the eastern Mediterranean, southern Turkey and in parts of southern Europe where it is probably naturalized. It occurs in stony places up to 2000m in altitude. The wild form is a very graceful plant and is well worth cultivating in warm sunny places or in a bulb frame. The nearest cultivars to the species in appearance are the Roman Hyacinths (these are nothing to do with the greenish-flowered *Hyacinthus romanus* which is now a *Bellevalia*). The range of large-flowered hyacinths now available is enormous, although possibly in the eighteenth and nineteenth centuries there were even more because of the popularity of the double ones which are rarely seen now.

The cultivars range from white and yellow to pale to deep blue and pale pink to deep red, colours not found in the true wild species. They are widely used for bedding displays and for forcing in bowls of fibre indoors. For this, very large bulbs are used and they can be 'prepared' while dormant by giving them a heat treatment for about five or six weeks at 70–78°F to encourage bud formation. Planted in the bowls in August and kept damp and cool, they can be left until flower buds are showing and then brought indoors. This is usually before Christmas with the heat-treated bulbs, but not until late winter with untreated ones. The smaller-flowered Roman Hyacinths can be forced as well and are to my mind more graceful and certainly more fragrant than their gigantic relatives. The cultivars can be grown out of doors, and although they become smaller in stature and flower-size they are long-lived and suitable for planting in sunny places among herbaceous plants or shrubs, where they flower in March or April.

Hymenocallis Amaryllidaceae

A large genus containing about 40 species, all from central and South America, and closely resembling the mainly Old World genus, *Pancratium*. The large white or yellow flowers are usually beautifully scented and the more prolific species may be used very effectively as pot or tub plants in a conservatory or planted out in temperate greenhouse beds. Some of the higher-altitude species from the Andes are nearly hardy in mild districts of south-west England but will not stand any prolonged cold damp periods. Like *Pancratium*, the flowers have six rather narrow perianth segments, basally joined into a long tube, and a distinct, sometimes very large, cup which is formed from the widely expanded and fused filaments of the stamens. The free part of each filament bends abruptly inwards so that the anthers all face into the centre of the flower rather than protruding from the cup. The cup is usually toothed or rather ragged at its mouth, and often flared outwards. Like many other Amaryllids, *Hymenocallis* species have several flowers in an umbel at the top of a naked peduncle and because of the long perianth tube the flowers are somewhat pendulous or arching outwards. The leaves are usually bright green, strap-shaped or narrowly lanceolate, and occasionally merge together at the base to form a stem, although this is not a true stem of course. I have not grown many of the species but it seems that they are best treated as summer-growing plants and kept dry and dormant in a warm place through the winter. Some of the more tropical species, which are not dealt with here, are nearly evergreen and therefore require water throughout the year, and a warm greenhouse.

H. amancaes Unusual in having bright yellow flowers, about one to eight in the umbel, on a 40–50cm stem. The staminal cup is up to 7cm in length and funnel-shaped with a rather jagged or fringed margin. Wild in Peru in stony and rocky places, 150–3000m altitude. It is one of the most beautiful, and one of the hardiest species, and has been hybridized with *H. narcissiflora* to produce creamy-yellow intermediates known as *H.* × *spofforthiae*. Spofforth was the home of W. Herbert who was probably one of the most knowledgeable gardener/

botanists of the early nineteenth century, certainly in the field of bulbous plants.
H. calathina See *H. narcissiflora*.
H. harrisiana Herb. Probably some of the most interesting species for gardeners
in the more northerly climates such as Britain are those coming from Mexico.
They are in general more compact in habit, are deciduous and summer bloom-
ing and occur at altitudes of up to 2500m. Although I do not suggest that they
would be hardy, they certainly should be less trouble, and my experience so far
has been that they can be stored dry for the winter under a greenhouse bench
along with the other 'summer-rainfall' bulbs from Mexico and the eastern Cape.
   H. harrisiana is a delicate plant compared to the robust *H. narcissiflora* and
produces three or four oblanceolate basal leaves which are often very short at
flowering time. The flower stem reaches 30–40cm in height and usually carries
two to four white, sweetly-scented flowers, these very spidery in appearance
with narrow segments and a small staminal cup. The perianth tube is about
8–10cm long and the segments 6–7cm long. It occurs on grassy hillsides at about
2000–2500m. *H. dillenii* has narrower leaves, usually only 2–3cm wide with a
tube 3·5–5cm long. *H. graminifolia* is, as its name suggests, a narrow-leaved
plant with about six linear leaves 0·5–1cm wide and a tube only 3·5–4cm long
but with a larger cup (3cm deep) than *H. dillenii* or *H. harrisiana* (1·5–2cm deep).
I now grow several of these Mexican species, thanks to James Bauml and Dr T.
Howard, Mrs Sally Walker and Caryn Ecker, but have not had them long
enough to be sure of their exact identification or of their cultural requirements.
H. narcissiflora (*H. calathina, Ismene calathina*) About 45–50cm in height when
in flower, with four to six substantial white flowers, shading to green at the base
of the segments and on the perianth tube. The funnel-shaped staminal cup is
very large, about 6cm long and flared outwards at its mouth to about 6cm in
diameter with six lobes, each jagged-toothed at the apex. The six perianth segments are about 1–1·5cm wide and only slightly longer than the cup. It occurs
mainly in the Peruvian Andes at about 3000m in fields and on stony hillsides,
and is nearly hardy in southern England although much better with protection.
A hybrid of *H. narcissiflora* known as *H.* 'Advance' is rather similar.

Iris Iridaceae

A very well-known genus especially the rhizomatous 'tall bearded' group, but
the bulbous species are equally attractive and have their place in gardens. Of
the taller species in the bulbous sections, it is mainly Section *Xiphium* which
concerns us here. Section *Juno* contains many beautiful plants but few of them
fall into the category of 'larger bulbs'. Some botanists split off the Xiphium and
Juno Sections as separate genera but I have not followed this and it is probably
a matter of very little importance to the horticulturalist.
Section Xiphium A well-known group, for it contains all of those useful plants

known as 'English', 'Spanish' and 'Dutch' Iris, which are so popular as cut flowers early in the year. The wild species, seven in number, are all confined to the western Mediterranean and form a small natural group within the genus *Iris*. The distinguishing features are (1) 'Falls' (outer perianth segments) with no beard (except *I. boissieri*), (2) a bulb covered with papery coats, (3) fibrous or slightly fleshy non-persistent roots, (4) channelled leaves and (5) erect 'Standards' (the inner three perianth segments), usually quite large and obvious, but very small in *I. serotina*. These species are attractive and on the whole easily grown, although some of them are rather tender and require bulb-frame cultivation. The hybrids and selections are more robust and easily grown. There is a great range of colours now and a perusal of the bulb retailers' catalogues will provide up-to-date information on those available, so I will deal only with the wild species and their variants.

Key to the I. xiphium group

A	Falls with a beard in the centre	*boissieri*
	Falls with no beard	B
B	Perianth tube more than 1cm long	C
	Perianth tube less than 1cm long	E
C	Flowers yellow	*juncea*
	Flowers red-purple, violet or blue	D
D	Standards slightly narrower than falls, rather round at tip; flowers red-purple	*filifolia*
	Standards distinctly narrower than falls, rather pointed at tip; flowers blue or violet	*tingitana*
E	Standards very small and hair-like; flowering in late summer (August)	*serotina*
	Standards large, 4–5cm long; flowering early to mid summer (May–June)	F
F	Lower half of the falls (the haft) at least 2·5cm wide; leaves appearing in spring	*xiphioides*
	Lower half of the falls less than 1cm wide; leaves appearing in autumn	*xiphium*

I. boissieri Unfortunately I have not had the opportunity to observe this species in the living state. It is an oddity in the group in that it has a thin beard of yellowish hairs on the falls, and the roots are slightly fleshy, more like those of a Juno Iris. 30–40cm in height with a single flower of deep violet-purple. Perianth tube 3–5cm long. Flowering in June. Northern Portugal and adjacent Spain, apparently rather local. It is very rare in cultivation, if indeed it is grown at all nowadays. It is said to be rather tender in Britain but I imagine that it would be not difficult in a bulb frame or cold greenhouse.

I. filifolia Grows up to 45cm in height with leaves varying from almost thread-like (in var. *filifolia*) to broadly linear (var. *latifolia*). Flowers one or two per inflorescence, rich red-violet with a yellow patch in the centre of the falls. Perianth tube 1–2·5cm long. Flowering in June. Southern Spain, Gibraltar, Morocco and Tangier. This beautiful species is not difficult if in a bulb frame. It is one of the excellent plants for which I have to thank the late Eliot Hodgkin. The long tube and richly coloured flowers distinguish this from any other species.

I. fontanesii See *I. tingitana*.

I. juncea A slender species about 30–40cm in height with very narrow leaves only 0·5–3mm wide. Flowers scented, bright yellow, usually two. Perianth tube 3·5–5cm long. Flowering in June. Southern Spain, Sicily, northern Africa. Another species which I have not grown. It is said to be rather tender and if so will require a greenhouse or bulb frame for protection. *I. juncea* can be recognized easily by its long slender flower tube, so need not be confused with the yellow forms of *I. xiphium*.

I. serotina This is a distinctive species which I now grow, thanks to Rosemary Strachey and John Marr who have given me bulbs in recent years. Reaches 60cm in height, with narrow basal leaves which die away before flowering time. The stem leaves are short and bract-like, becoming brown before the flowers open. Flowers violet-blue with a yellow line in the centre of the falls. The standards are reduced to 1cm or less and are bristle-like, making this quite different from any other *Iris* of this group. Perianth tube 0·5–1cm long. Flowering in August. South-east Spain, in Jaen province where it grows in the mountains in scrub. My plants have been grown successfully in a bulb frame and in deep pots in a cool greenhouse. Although a very interesting species, *I. serotina* does not rank as one of the most attractive since the whole plant looks practically dead by the time it flowers in late summer.

I. taitii See *I. xiphium*.

I. tingitana A robust species up to 60cm in height with long arching silvery-green leaves. Flowers large, one to three produced in each set of spathes, pale to deep blue, or violet-blue (in var. *fontanesii*). Perianth tube long and slender. Flowering February to May. Wild in Morocco and Algeria. This is a somewhat tender species and I have never been very successful with it out of doors. Sir Frederick Stern had fine clumps of it in his garden at Highdown in Sussex, where it grew in full sun on a hot, dry, chalky soil. The variety *fontanesii* flowers slightly later than var. *tingitana* and is a more slender plant with darker flowers. Var. *mellori* was described by Collingwood Ingram in 1973 as a variety of *I. fontanesii*. It is a very robust *Iris* up to 98cm in height with purple flowers and is said to differ from *I. tingitana* in having a very rounded blade to the falls (more pointed in *I. tingitana*) and from var. *fontanesii* in being much taller and having purple coloured flowers. I have not grown the plant, but Captain Ingram recommends lifting the bulbs in summer and keeping them on a sunny shelf for three months before replanting. It grows in Morocco in wet fields. Hybrids between

I. tingitana and *I. xiphium* have given rise to the race of garden plants known as Dutch Iris.

I. xiphioides English Iris. Another strong-growing species usually up to 60cm in height with long leaves not appearing until spring, up to 65cm long, greyish-white on the upper surface. Flowers large, usually two in each set of spathes, violet-blue with a central yellow patch on the falls. Perianth tube about 0·5cm long. The falls have wide 'wings' on the lower half, a significant point when comparing this species with *I. xiphium*. Flowering in June–July. North-west Spain, French and Spanish Pyrenees in damp grassy places. An easy species to grow in the open border, preferably in a position which does not dry out too much. There are many garden forms with variously coloured flowers, all in shades of blue, violet or purple, or a pure white, but never yellow.

I. xiphium Spanish Iris. This is probably the most variable of all the species, especially in flower colour. Grows up to 50cm in height, and sometimes more, with leaves present during winter. One or two flowers are produced within each set of spathes. The colour of wild forms is usually violet with an orange or yellow blotch in the centre of the falls, but can be wholly yellow or white. The lower part of the falls has no wide 'wing', as in *I. xiphioides*, and instead the margins of this 'haft', as it is called, are more or less parallel. Perianth tube only 1–3mm long. Flowering April–May. Occurs wild in south-west France, Corsica, Italy, Spain, Portugal, Morocco, Algeria and Tunis. Several varieties have been described, depending upon the colour: var. *xiphium* has blue, mauve or violet flowers; var. *battandieri* is white with an orange ridge on the falls and comes from Morocco and Algeria; var. *lusitanica* from Portugal has pure yellow or bronze flowers and is a robust grower; var. *praecox* flowers in April, a little earlier than the majority of forms; and var. *taitii* rather later.

I. xiphium and its varieties present no great problem in gardens for it requires only a sunny well-drained position. The Dutch Iris are hybrids between *I. xiphium* and *I. tingitana*, and probably *I. xiphioides* also. They flower rather earlier than true *I. xiphium* and are often forced in cool greenhouses for use as cut flowers. The colour range of these hybrids is very wide, from white to yellow and bronze and pale blue to deep mauve.

Section Juno A group of beautiful bulbous Iris, unfortunately not generally easy to cultivate. However, some of the larger species, which are the ones we are concerned with here, are not at all difficult and can be grown in the open in sunny well-drained soils. Hardiness is not a problem for they mostly inhabit areas with a very cold winter. Whether they are grown under glass or in the open it should be remembered that they like a dryish summer. Unlike the majority of *Iris* species, the inner perianth segments, or standards, are not large and erect but are considerably smaller than the falls and horizontal or deflexed. The roots of Juno Iris are thick and fleshy, radiating from the base of the bulb. These should be treated carefully when lifting bulbs as they are very brittle and can be broken off very easily. The bulb will, however, survive if they are removed but might be a little weaker. It has often been stated that these roots will form new bulbs if they are detached and planted. I have not found this to be so but that does not mean it is not worth trying. The leaves of Juno Iris are channelled and produced in a distichous fan, sometimes all together near the base of the stem, but in the taller species spread out up the stem with gaps between them.

Some species can be increased by bulb division, but undoubtedly the best method of propagation is by seed, which takes three to five years to produce a flowering plant. In my experience the seed is best sown before the autumn and then left out in the open to receive any frosts, which assist germination. After this they can be moved under glass to protect them from excess moisture and kept growing for as long as possible into the late spring and summer. Many of the taller species come from Russian Central Asia and are scarcely known in the west, if in cultivation at all. I have only included those which are known to me – not necessarily cultivated by me unfortunately.

I. aitchisonii One of the most easterly-occurring of all the Juno Iris. Up to 36cm in height with distinct gaps between the very narrow leaves which vary from 0·3–0·8cm wide. Inflorescence sometimes branched. Flowers one to three, which can be yellow, yellow and brown, or purple. Standards reflexed, 1·3–2·6cm long. Falls 3·5–5·5cm long, with the lower portion broadly winged. Grows in dampish, often grassy, places but very dry in summer at about 1000m in western Pakistan and eastern Afghanistan. I have not yet flowered *I. aitchisonii*, although bulbs and seeds sent to me by Dr Nasir of Rawalpindi grew well in their first year after arrival. It probably needs cold dry winters, a short growing season and a long hot rest period in summer.

I. aucheri (*I. fumosa*, *I. sindjarensis*) Up to 40cm in height with the stem hidden by the broad leaves in the flowering stage; leaves glossy green on the upper surface, 2·5–4·5cm broad. Flowers one to six in the axils of the upper leaves, blue to nearly white with a yellow crest on the falls which are 4·5–5cm long with a wide wing on the lower portion. Standards horizontal or slightly deflexed, about 2·5cm long. In rocky places and on ledges at 550–2100m in northern Iraq, northern Syria, south-east Turkey and western Iran. Not a difficult species to grow in pots or a bulb frame but not particularly successful out of doors, at least in south-east England. The form distributed by the firm of van Tubergen is especially good in its blue coloration.

I. bucharica (*I. orchioides* of gardens) One of the best-known Juno species and easily grown. Up to 45cm in height, rarely a little more. Leaves up to 4cm wide, completely hiding the stem at flowering time, glossy green. Flowers up to seven in the axils of the upper leaves, varying from pale yellow with white styles to deep yellow (in 'I. orchioides'). The crest is deeper yellow and usually has brownish, purplish or deep green markings on either side. Falls about 4cm long with no wing on the lower part. Standards white or yellow, horizontal or deflexed, 1·5–2cm long. North-east Afghanistan and Tadjikistan up to 2400m on open rocky hillsides. Both the yellow and white form and the deep yellow 'I.

orchioides' are easy to grow out of doors in a well-drained sunny spot, and are completely hardy. In Afghanistan both forms have been collected in mixed populations by Paul and Polly Furse, showing that they are merely colour variants of one species. The true *I. orchioides* of Carrière appears to be a different species from Russia, for it has wings on the haft of the falls. I have never seen a living specimen of this.

I. cycloglossa The most extraordinary species of all the Junos and one of the most beautiful. Described in 1958 by Per Wendelbo and introduced into cultivation by him. Up to 56cm in height with narrow leaves up to 1·5cm broad, widely scattered up the stem. Inflorescence with a terminal flower, or branched, an unusual feature in Junos. Flowers one to three, of a clear pale blue-lilac with a white zone and a yellow patch around the shallow ridge in the centre of the falls. Falls with a large, nearly round, blade 3·5–4cm in diameter and a wide wing on the lower portion. Standards erect, oblanceolate, about 4cm long. Grows wild in a very limited area of south-west Afghanistan in wet grass-filled depressions at 1450–1700m. *I. cycloglossa* is not very closely related to any other Juno. It has upright, relatively large standards, a branched inflorescence and grows in wet places, whereas most others prefer dry stony hills or sandy areas. The bulb which Mr Michael Hoog kindly gave me was one of those collected by Wendelbo, Hedge and Eckberg, no 7727. This has increased to four in as many years and is very easy to grow. Prior to 1976 I grew it in a very deep pot in a cold frame but in 1976 planted it out in the open. In 1977 it flowered beautifully and appears to be perfectly tolerant of the English weather. It is certainly a most beautiful species, and the flowers are clove scented.

I. drepanophylla See *I. kopetdagensis*.

I. fumosa See *I. aucheri*.

I. kopetdagensis The tallest of the green-flowered species, growing up to 35cm in height with 1–2·5cm wide greyish-green leaves which are strongly curved and tend to be fairly closely arranged on the stem at flowering time. Flowers three to nine, greenish with a very raised yellow-orange crest on the falls which are about 4–5cm long. The lower part of the falls has nearly parallel margins with no wide wing, but the margins are slightly upturned. Standards 0·5–1cm long, very narrow and pointed. It occurs on dry slopes between 1000–3000m in northeast Iran, north-west Afghanistan and the adjacent Kopet Dagh mountains of Russia. My bulbs of this were introduced by Paul and Polly Furse in the 1960s, and although I still have it I find it a difficult species to flower. *I. drepanophylla* is superficially very similar. It is slightly smaller generally and the flower is yellow and more slender. The main difference is that the margins of the haft turn downwards, not up as in *I. kopetdagensis*.

Iris magnifica The best hardy Juno for outdoors. Up to 60cm with broad glossy leaves up the stem and 4–7 flowers in their axils. Flowers lilac (white in var. *alba*) with an orange spot in the centre of the widely winged falls. Standards spoon-shaped, 2cm long. Rocky slopes in the Russian Pamir-Alai.

I. warleyensis Grows 20–40cm in height, with scattered leaves 1·5–3cm wide, somewhat sickle-shaped. Flowers two to five, with falls 4–5·5cm long, not winged in the lower half. The colour is a strong violet with a deep yellow blotch around the whitish ridge. Standards roughly three-lobed, 1·2–2cm long, violet. Russian Pamir-Alai mountains on stony slopes. A striking species with its strong violet and yellow contrasts and not particularly difficult in well-drained sunny, preferably alkaline, soil. The late E. B. Anderson grew this very well in his Cotswold garden.

Leopoldia Liliaceae

Usually included in *Muscari*, as a section of that genus, but the species are very distinct and there is no need for confusion. Leopoldias are on the whole rather dull compared with the Grape Hyacinths, for their fully open flowers are usually some shade of brownish, greenish, purplish or yellow. However, a few have a very bright cluster of sterile flowers at the apex of the inflorescence and I certainly can find a place for them in the garden for they flower rather later than most bulbs, in June. There are about ten species, widely distributed in Mediterranean Europe eastwards to Iran. They are characterized by being bulbous, with basal linear leaves and a raceme of small, rather tubular flowers with very short perianth segments. The upper flowers are sterile and are often on long pedicels, and brightly coloured. They are easily grown in a sunny well-drained site.

L. comosa This is the most widespread and well-known species, sometimes called the Tassel Hyacinth. The stem can reach about 60cm in height and carries very many pale-brownish fertile flowers with white or yellow perianth lobes. The purple sterile flowers are on much longer pedicels and are held upright, whereas the fertile flowers are carried horizontally. Even the pedicels of the sterile flowers are coloured so that this can be quite a showy plant if grown in a clump. It is a very common plant around the Mediterranean in fields and grassy places, never at high altitudes. I find it perfectly hardy in Surrey and it increases well by offsets to produce sizeable flowering clumps. Even better is the white form, in which the sterile flowers are all white. This shows up best against a darkish background and looks attractive in association with groups of the tall, deep-purple Alliums such as *A. aflatunense*. There is also a mutation of *L. comosa* called var. *monstrosa* in which the flowers have become sterile and converted into a feathery mass. *L. tenuiflora* is a separate species, rather similar to *L. comosa*, but it has blackish perianth lobes.

L. longipes A very striking species which so much impressed Paul and Polly Furse on one of their expeditions that they dubbed it the 'Blue-Hot Poker'. It grows to about 60cm in height and the flowering portion of the stem can be as much as 30cm. The inflorescence is very dense in the early stages, with the tightly packed buds bright purple, but later it becomes looser, with the spaced-out

Nerine bowdenii, a first-rate autumn-flowering bulb for a sunny wall

Pancratium illyricum is hardy only in very mild areas and is best suited to a cool greenhouse

Trillium sessile is most suitable for a woodland garden

Veltheimia bracteata, a good pot plant for the conservatory (below)
Veltheimia bracteata 'Rosalba', a cultivar with slightly different colouring (below right)

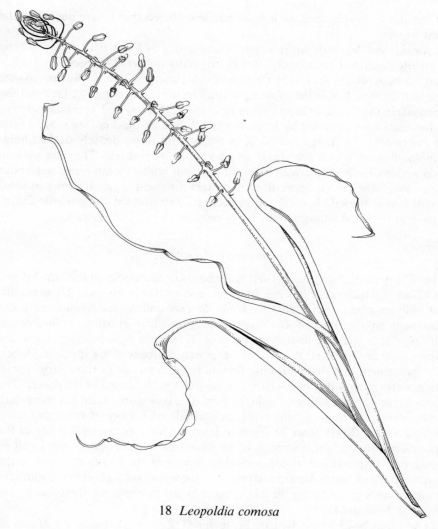

18 *Leopoldia comosa*

flowers on 3cm pedicels. As they reach maturity, the flowers become brownish, greenish or yellowish with black perianth segments, but the sterile upper flowers remain a bright violet-blue. Even in fruit the plant is rather dramatic, for the lower pedicels carrying the large capsules elongate to about 7cm to give the whole conical fruiting head a spread of about 15cm wide and 30cm long. It is a native of the southern Caucasus, central and eastern Turkey, northern Iraq and Iran in fields and vineyards, up to 2000m altitude. I have found it to be most impressive in a bulb frame but admit to not having experimented with it outside. It is a variable plant and I have seen forms in the wild with greenish buds instead of the showy purple ones, so it must be remembered that I have described the best form.

L. massayana A poorly-known species and as far as I can tell it has not been formally described botanically. It was originally collected by Siehe in Turkey and has been offered for sale by the firm of van Tubergen, but its wild provenance was not known. It was therefore surprising to see it flowering not far from the roadside in the Cilician Gates Pass in June 1965 (Mathew and Tomlinson 4468). It has since been collected by J. Allison and P. Ball on the Ala Dag range a little to the east of this. It reaches 30cm in height with many densely packed long-tubular flowers which are sessile or on very short pedicels. They are pink in bud and greenish-yellow with blackish perianth segments later, and are about 8mm long. The sterile upper flowers remain pinkish-purple. It grows in scree conditions in the wild but will accept ordinary well-drained soil in a bulb frame. I have not yet had enough bulbs to try outside.

Leucocoryne Liliaceae

The 'Glory of the Sun', *L. ixioides*, is the best-known species in this small genus of 12, all of which occur in Chile from sea level to 1000m altitude. These beautiful bulbous plants are related to *Milla, Ipheion* and *Nothoscordum*, all Latin American counterparts of *Allium* and having the same umbellate inflorescence, although it is reduced to only a few large flowers in *Leucocoryne*. These are white, blue or violet and have a distinct perianth tube with six spreading lobes. The prominent and distinguishing feature is the presence of three large sterile stamens forming rather club-shaped staminodes in the centre of the flower. The three fertile ones are hidden within the tube. The leaves are linear, not more than 5mm wide, and these in my experience usually die away at flowering time, leaving a bare flower stem 20–60cm in height. I have grown only a few of the species, but they all seem to require the same treatment. They are not hardy in south-east England but would probably survive in the south-west and in the warmer parts of North America. Being from the winter rainfall region of southern America, they grow during the winter months and flower in my frost-free greenhouse in March–May.

The genus has been revised by Professor O. Zöllner in *Anales del Museo de Historia Natural de Valparaiso* No 5 (1972).

L. coquimbensis has up to ten flowers in the umbel, variable in colour but usually pale bluish-violet fading to a white zone in the centre and a small green 'eye'. The tube is about 1–1·2cm long and the oblong segments about 2–2·5cm long giving a flower diameter of up to 5·5cm. The sterile stamens are rather conical, deep yellow. It occurs in Coquimbo, Valparaiso and Aconcagua provinces of Chile. A white variety, *alba*, has been described by Professor Zöllner. This is a beautiful species and so far has proved to be the most reliable in cultivation, flowering well for nearly two months and very sweetly scented.

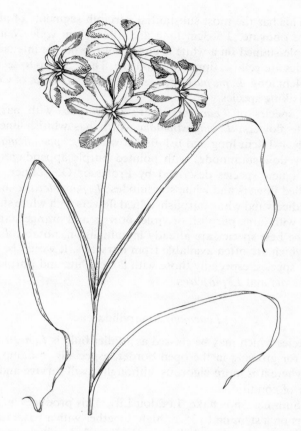

19 *Leucocoryne ixioides*

L. ixioides The best-known species and usually fairly easy to obtain. It is similar in stature to the above species, and differs mainly in its flower characters. The segments are more spear-shaped and the sterile stamens are white and rather slender. The colour is usually pale blue but it can vary from white to purplish-blue. *L. ixioides* occurs in the provinces of Santiago, Aconcagua, Valparaiso and Coquimbo. In commerce *L. ixioides* var. *odorata* is sometimes offered, this being the sweetly scented plant introduced by Clarence Elliott in the 1930s. Zöllner keeps this as a separate species, *L. odorata*, which has much shorter pedicels (less than 2cm; 3–6·5 cm in *L. ixioides*) with pale, smaller flowers. It grows wild in Valparaiso province.

L. macropetala is a pure-white-flowered species with narrow lanceolate, very pointed segments and yellow staminodes. It produces up to 12 flowers on a 15–20cm stem. Known from Coquimbo and Atacama provinces.

L. purpurea This has the most substantial perianth segments of all the species, since they are obovate, 2·5–3cm long and about 1cm wide. While fresh, the colour is purple-stained on a white ground, but the purple intensifies with age. The staminodes are yellow, tipped with purple. There are up to seven flowers on pedicels 2·5–4cm long. *L. purpurea* grows wild in the province of Coquimbo and is the most striking species.

The other species of *Leucocoryne* are *L. alliacea*, with narrow-petalled, greenish-white flowers; *L. angustipetala* which has whitish linear-lanceolate segments only 1–1·4cm long and 0·1–0·3cm wide; *L. appendiculata* with white flowers and yellow staminodes with pointed purple appendages at the apex; *L. conferta*, a new species described by Professor O. Zöllner, having white narrow-petalled flowers and white staminodes; *L. pauciflora*, a smallish species with short pedicels and white purplish-veined flowers with white staminodes and *L. violascens* with large purplish or violet flowers and orange staminodes.

Some of the best species are already in cultivation, notably *L. ixioides* and *L. odorata*, which are often available from nurseries. It would be interesting to try the other species, especially those with large white and purple flowers such as *L. macropetala* and *L. purpurea*.

Leucojum Amaryllidaceae

The only species which may be classed as a taller bulb is *L. aestivum*, a reliable hardy plant for growing in the open border, especially in damp situations on heavy soils where it is more vigorous, although it will survive and flower under a wide range of conditions.

L. aestivum Summer Snowflake, Loddon Lily. This produces an umbel of two to five flowers on a stem up to 35cm high, together with a basal tuft of daffodil-like leaves; flowers pendulous, bell-shaped, about 3–4cm in diameter, white with green markings near the apex of each of the six equal segments. Occurs wild in south-east England, Ireland and central Europe to the Caucasus, flowering in April–May in Britain.

The selection 'Gravetye Giant' is a very robust form which can reach 90cm when growing near water. Var. *pulchellum* scarcely differs from the typical plant and is not worth recognition as a separate entity. *L. aestivum* increases well by bulb division and forms large clumps which can be divided at any time of year, although the bulbs should never be dried out too much. It is attractive when grown in areas of rough grass.

Lilium Liliaceae

Probably the best-known genus in the whole of this large family, the 90 species all being beautiful and worthy of cultivation. Since they mostly occur in northern temperate or mountain areas from western Europe east through the

20 *Leucojum aestivum*

Caucasus, Himalayas and China to Japan and North America, the majority
are hardy in Britain. Several of the eastern Asian species and a few from the
southern states of the USA are, however, tender and are normally grown as
greenhouse plants. Lilies have scaly bulbs and leafy stems, the leaves either being
alternate or in whorls and usually rather narrowly lanceolate or linear. Some
species produce a tuft of roots from the stem just as it emerges from the bulb,
these stem-roots partly acting as extra support and partly of course to obtain
more nourishment for the developing stem. In some species stolons are produced
from the parent bulb giving rise to young bulbs at their tips, while in others the
bulb has the ability to elongate sideways and can thus travel horizontally
through the soil. Bulblets are produced in the axils of the leaves or on the stem
at ground level in a few species, this being a useful method of propagation.

The flowers of lilies vary in shape and colour enormously from species to species, allowing the genus to be divided up on the basis of perianth shape. The arrangement of flowers on the stem can be solitary or racemose, sometimes with the raceme so condensed that the flowers appear to arise in an umbel-like way from the same point. The arrangement of the species in Woodcock & Stearn's *Lilies of the World**is easy to follow, although it must be accepted that the grouping of *Lilium* species into completely 'watertight' compartments is more or less impossible, there always being a few species which fall between groups or are difficult to place. The four groups recognized in this authoritative book are (1) *Leucolirion*, which houses the large trumpet lilies such as *L. longiflorum* and *L. regale*; (2) *Archelirion* for the large wide-open-flowered species, *L. auratum*, in which the perianth segments are broadest below the middle; (3) *Pseudo-lirium*, the orange or red-flowered ones with the flower cup- or bowl-shaped and upright; and (4) *Martagon*, for those with flowers having sharply recurring perianth segments and pendulous flowers, the Turk's Cap Lilies.

In the following list of species I have selected those species which are well known and available in cultivation, or are my particular favourites, since I cannot hope to include them all here. The Groups as described above are indicated by the letters L, A, P or M – denoting *Leucolirion*, *Archelirion*, *Pseudolirium*, or *Martagon* – in brackets after the specific epithet. I do not propose to deal with any of the numerous hybrids since space does not allow this.

Cultivation

Much has been, and will continue to be written about the cultivation of lilies and I have no new magic formula to solve your problems! I think it is sufficient to say that most lilies are not plants for dry hot situations, so in general do not plant them along a south-facing wall. They do not like waterlogged soils, so if the site is on heavy poorly-drained clay it must be made lighter with coarse sand and peat or leafmould. There are of course notable exceptions to these general statements and I will mention these under the species concerned. The bulbs should be planted at about 10–20cm deep in general, the stem-rooting species being planted at the deepest level.

Virus disease is, I suppose, one of the worst problems with lily cultivation and if one has a healthy stock then attempt to keep it that way by spraying against aphids regularly during the growing season, since it is these pests which not only disfigure the plants but can also transfer virus from diseased to healthy stock. Seedlings raised from virus-infected plants are usually free from the disease, so this is another way of avoiding the problem, although if badly virused the old plants are usually too weak or malformed to produce seeds anyway.

Being summer-flowering, lilies are very suited to a position where they will

* Country Life Ltd. London 1950

brighten up areas which are otherwise dull at that time of year. Thus it is of little use planting them amongst tall herbaceous plants or in rose beds but they are ideal among rhododendrons or camellias where they can take over after spring bulbs such as daffodils have left open spaces. If the natural soil is totally unsuitable, areas can be prepared for lilies with the addition of humus and sand, or they can be grown very effectively in tubs on a terrace or patio. The only point to remember is that nourishment is required and an annual dressing with a granular slow-release general fertilizer is essential in spring. Re-potting should take place every other year in late winter or early spring before the roots become very active. Most lilies flower in Britain in mid to late summer.

L. amabile (M) Stem-rooting. 45–90cm in height with many scattered narrowly lanceolate leaves up to 4cm long and 1cm wide. The raceme carries up to ten pendulous flowers of a rich red spotted with black, with the segments rolled right back. The anthers are chocolate coloured. *L. amabile* is a Korean plant and is thus very hardy in Britain. It is easily grown from seed and must be grown in a well-drained soil, but I have never known it to be very long-lived. *L. amabile* var. *luteum* is a yellow-flowered variant which has arisen in cultivation.

L. auratum (A) One of the most well-known species, commonly known as the Golden-rayed Hill Lily of Japan. Stem rooting. It grows up to about 150cm or even more in cultivation, the stem carrying scattered, leathery, dark green, narrowly ovate leaves up to 20cm long and 3·5cm wide. The number of flowers varies enormously but is usually about five to ten, carried in a raceme. Each strongly fragrant flower is 25–30cm in diameter and is a wide open funnel or bowl-shape with the tips of the segments rolled back and the segments broad and overlapping in the lower half. The ground colour is white with a yellow band along the centre of each segment and the flower is spotted internally with crimson. Variants of this exist in colours ranging from plain white to crimson-banded, with varying degrees of spotting. It occurs in Japan, on sharply-drained hillsides amongst shrubs and grasses. In cultivation in Britain it is perfectly hardy and requires a semi-shady position in a light freely-draining soil. It does require plenty of moisture in the growing season and should be mulched with peat or leafmould each year to help to keep the soil rich in humus. Unfortunately this species is very susceptible to virus and the stems, leaves and flowers become terribly distorted. The only course is to burn the infected bulbs and obtain new stock, or grow bulbs from seed. Aphids should be controlled on all lilies during the growing season since they are responsible for spreading the virus. Named varieties of *L. auratum* include *virginale*, pure white; *rubrum*, with a crimson, instead of a yellow stripe; *rubro-vittatum* is similar to this; *platyphyllum*, a very large-flowered variety with a yellow band and less spotting than the usual wild form; *pictum* with a crimson stripe and very heavy crimson spotting.

L. canadense (M) A beautiful graceful lily which is one of my own favourites, although at present I do not have it. It has a curious bulb which consists of a mass of small scales and it creeps horizontally in a stoloniferous manner. The stem is up to 130cm in height, carrying whorled lanceolate leaves up to 15cm long and 2cm broad and an umbellate inflorescence of up to 20 flowers, although in cultivation in Britain it rarely produces more than ten. The more vigorous specimens tend to produce a whorl of flowers below the terminal umbel. Each 7–10cm diameter flower is carried on a long pedicel which is curved upwards almost to the vertical and then turns over to hold the flower in a pendent position. The bell shape is not typical of the martagon section, since the segments only flare outwards rather than rolling back on themselves. The colour varies from pale yellow to orange and red, usually spotted blackish internally. It grows in the eastern parts of North America in damp grassy places or light woodland. In cultivation it is best if given a moist position with plenty of peat or leafmould, although at the same time the drainage must be reasonably good. The best plants I ever grew were in a raised peat bed in semi-shade.

L. candidum (L) Although generally grouped with the large white trumpet lilies, the Madonna Lily is so distinct in its widely-flaring flowers and over-wintering basal leaves that it is sometimes placed in a section of its own. *L. candidum* is possibly the longest cultivated lily, certainly since the times of the ancient Cretan and Egyptian civilizations for it is depicted on vases and murals. It is now very difficult to say which is its native provenance, but most probably it occurs wild in the eastern Mediterranean as far west as Greece.

It is not stem-rooting and the bulbs are best planted with their tips only 2cm beneath the surface. The basal leaves are oblanceolate, up to 20cm long and 5cm wide and form a rosette in autumn which overwinters and dies away at flowering time. The flower stem is 100–150cm in height and is nearly covered in the lower part with lanceolate rather erect leaves, these becoming more spaced out higher up the stem. The flowers are carried in a short raceme of up to 15, each being widely bell-shaped and facing outwards.

Although it used to be a very common plant in British gardens it is less often seen nowadays. It seems to grow best in well-drained alkaline soils, the sort of place where bearded *Iris* flourish. I have seen it in Greece growing in clumps on the flat roof of a house in the Peloponnese, flowering magnificently in a clod of soil. The lesson to be gained is that it must have plenty of sun. Because the bulbs begin to grow and produce leaves in autumn they must be planted at the end of the summer.

L. carniolicum (M) A beautiful Turk's Cap Lily with slender stems 60–120cm in height. The numerous, 5–7cm long leaves are alternate, narrowly lanceolate and spread out horizontally from the stem. The pendulous flowers are all produced at about the same point, although the inflorescence is not an umbel, and there are usually two to four or, rarely, up to six. The shape is a typical martagon-type with the segments rolled right back. In var. *carniolicum* the colour is light red or orange-red and the protruding anthers are red. It is an alpine or subalpine plant of Yugoslavia, western Bulgaria, Hungary and Rumania and I have seen it both in lightly-wooded situations and in short alpine turf, depending upon the altitude. Var. *jankae* has yellow flowers spotted with black, but the anthers are reddish. It occurs in more southerly parts of the range of the species. Var. *albanicum* is also a yellow-flowered form which has glabrous leaves, whereas in var. *carniolicum* and var. *jankae* they are hairy on the veins of the undersurface. The anthers are cinnamon-coloured. It occurs in Albania and adjacent northern Greece. All the forms are stem-rooting. I have not found *L. carniolicum* an easy species to grow for it needs that interesting combination of a free-draining, preferably alkaline, soil which is fairly heavy. A top-dressing of leafmould is necessary each year.

L. cernuum (M) A graceful species only 30–60cm in height with many very narrow 15–18cm long leaves packed quite tightly on the central region of the stem with few at the base or apex. The one to seven scented pendulous flowers are carried on long slender pedicels and are of a strong purplish pink with deep purple spots towards the centre. The segments curl right back leaving the purplish anthers protruding prominently. It is stem-rooting. In the wild it grows in grassy places and in scrub in Korea, north to eastern Russia. Although I have not grown this species it is said to be easily raised from seed which produces flowering bulbs in about three years. It is suitable for rock gardens and should be given a well-drained soil mixture of sandy or gritty loam and leafmould.

L. chalcedonicum (M) A long-cultivated lily, certainly since the seventeenth century. Even so it is rarely seen in gardens for it is not the easiest of plants to grow. It grows 80–120cm in height with crowded silver-edged leaves which clothe the stem all the way up. The lower, longest ones usually spread outwards somewhat but the upper shorter ones are erect and press against the stem. The five to ten brilliant red Turk's Cap flowers have the segments rolled right back on themselves and are pendulous. The anthers are reddish. *L. chalcedonicum* is not stem-rooting; in the wild it occurs on the mountains of Greece. It seems to do best in sunny positions in alkaline soils, such as the chalky gardens of the South Downs can provide. *L. heldreichii* is usually regarded as being a variant of *L. chalcedonicum* and is also a native of Greece. It is said to have tomato-red flowers with broad perianth segments, but I am not familiar with the plant in the living state. *L. chalcedonicum* var. *maculatum* is a variant with black-spotted flowers and is reputed to be easier to grow.

L. concolor (P) A slender, graceful lily 30–90cm in height with rather scattered linear or linear lanceolate leaves 7–9cm in length and about 1·5cm wide. The three to ten flattish, starry flowers are produced in an umbel or a compact raceme and are held upright on shortish pedicels. The colour of the typical form is a brilliant shiny red without any spotting but other forms exist in which the flowers are deep-red spotted on a red ground, brownish spotted on a yellow ground or are plain yellow. *L. concolor* is stem-rooting. In the wild it grows in grassy places or in scrub in rather open situations in central China. It is not a difficult lily to grow, given a well-drained soil and a sunny situation, but is fairly short-lived. It is easily raised from seed and it is wise to keep a small supply of young plants growing on.

L. croceum (P) (*L. bulbiferum, L. aurantiacum*). The common upright-flowered orange lily of Europe. It is a variable species from 30–150cm in height with many scattered, narrowly lanceolate leaves up to 15cm long and 1·5cm wide, sometimes bearing bulbils in their axils. The umbellate inflorescence usually bears only a few flowers, but up to 50 have been recorded in some forms. The erect flowers are bright orange and cup-shaped, some colour variants having deeper reddish-brown spotting within the cup. It is a stem-rooting lily. *L. croceum* is a widespread plant in the wild from the Pyrenees to Hungary and Czechoslovakia, occurring in light woodland and in grassy scrub-covered hillsides. In cultivation it presents no problems and grows well in full sun or slight shade in most types of soil.

L. dauricum (P) A stocky species growing not more than 60cm in height with a stoloniferous stem running a short distance underground before emerging. It bears scattered, narrowly lanceolate leaves up to 15cm long and 1·5–2·5cm wide. The one to five upward-facing flowers are of an open bowl-shape and are reddish orange, spotted with deep brownish-red in the centre. It is a stem-rooting lily. *L. wilsonii* is very similar, with clear orange flowers, and is probably a variety of *L. dauricum*. In *L. wilsonii* var. *luteum* the flowers are yellow spotted with black. *L. pardinum* is probably a synonym of *L. wilsonii*. They occur wild in eastern Russia, Japan and Korea. *L. dauricum* is an easily grown lily suitable for a sunny rock garden or border. It is best in a well-drained soil in full sun.

L. davidii (M) A tall, graceful lily up to 140cm in height with the stems slender and bearing very many scattered, narrowly linear leaves up to 10cm long and less than 0·5cm wide. The five to 20 pendulous Turk's Cap flowers are carried on long pedicels which stand out horizontally from the stem, 10–15cm in length. The flowers are bright orange with raised black spots towards the centre. It is stem-rooting and often produces bulblets on the stem just below the soil surface. Var. *willmottiae* is a vigorous form with up to 30 reddish-orange flowers on slightly deflexed pedicels. Var. *unicolor* has unspotted flowers. Other variants have been raised in cultivation, some with yellowish flowers. *L. davidii* is comparatively easy to grow in a sunny border which has had plenty of leafmould worked into the soil. Plenty of moisture should be available in the growing season.

L. duchartrei (*L. farreri*) (M) Farrer's Marble Martagon. This beautiful lily has a stoloniferous habit, the stems often creeping horizontally for some distance and each producing a new bulb so that it is capable of producing large colonies. The stem reaches 60–100cm in height and bears deep green, usually lanceolate, scattered leaves 5–10cm long and 1–1·5cm wide. The one to 12 smallish pendulous flowers are carried in an umbel, or sometimes in a compact raceme, and are white with purple spotting and veining, becoming reddish-purple as they mature. *L. duchartrei* is stem-rooting. It occurs wild in western China in Kansu, Yunnan and Szechuan. The most successful colony I ever grew was in a peat garden in Surrey, the small bulbs being planted in a bed shaded by a large beech tree in soil consisting mainly of stony loam enriched with leafmould and sedge peat. There are several related species which should possibly be considered as forms of *L. duchartrei*. *L. taliense* has a loosely racemose inflorescence giving it a rather different appearance to the typically umbellate inflorescence of *L. duchartrei*. The habit of growth and the flowers are very similar. *L. lankongense* also has a racemose inflorescence and its flowers have a pink ground colour and are produced rather later in the season, in August. *L. wardii* from south-east Tibet is a robust plant with stems up to 150cm and leaves up to 2cm wide. The pink, dark-spotted flowers are arranged in a raceme, on long horizontal pedicels, usually 10–15cm long. It is an easy plant to grow in semi-shade in leafy soil.

L. formosanum (L) A well-known and easy trumpet lily, unfortunately not one of the hardiest. The stems vary greatly in height from 30–150cm, the more dwarf forms from higher altitudes being hardier here in Britain. The very narrow linear leaves are 10–20cm in length and about 1cm wide and are usually very numerous. Although the strongly scented flowers are often solitary in the plants I have grown, there can be three or four and, rarely, up to ten. They are trumpet shaped, with recurving tips to the segments, usually about 15–20cm in length. Internally the colour is pure white but the exterior is flushed with wine-purple to a varying degree, the more dwarf forms usually having the most colour. *L. formosanum* is stem-rooting. It is, as the name shows, a native of Taiwan where it grows on grassy hill slopes from sea level to over 3000m. *L. formosanum* is easily grown in a cool greenhouse where it will flower from seed in about nine months. I have grown it successfully out of doors in Surrey but it is not reliably hardy. It makes a beautiful pot plant and I have used it for a display in a large tub on the patio. The high altitude variant, collected by Mr W. R. Price and given the name var. *pricei*, is much hardier than the lowland forms and can be grown in a sunny border. It is usually about 30–60cm in height with solitary flowers which are purplish on the exterior.

L. giganteum See genus *Cardiocrinum*.

L. hansonii (M) A fine easy lily growing about 100–150cm in height with whorls of 2cm wide elliptical or oblanceolate dark green leaves. The three to ten pendulous flowers are deep yellow with numerous brown spots towards the centre. The segments recurve but do not roll inwards as in many of the Martagon group and are very thick and substantial. It is a stem-rooting lily, growing wild in Korea and Japan. In cultivation it requires only plenty of humus and a semi-shady position. It is very hardy and increases well by vegetative means.

L. henryi (M) A graceful, very easy and inexpensive lily. It reaches 150–180cm in height with purplish arching stems and glossy deep-green leaves which are lanceolate on the lower part, about 15cm long by 3cm wide, becoming shorter and broader on the upper part of the stem. The ten to 20 or more flowers are pendulous, carried in a loose raceme on long horizontal pedicels, and are like a large Martagon in shape with the segments rolled right back until the tips touch the pedicel. The colour is deep orange with very dark spots in the lower parts of the segments which are also covered in this region with numerous protruberances. It is a native of central China and is stem-rooting. *L. henryi* is a lime-loving lily and does particularly well in a chalky soil with leafmould added, although it will thrive in most soils in light shade, providing it is not too acid. The form which I grew for many years had bulbils in the leaf axils but it is more usual for this species to produce small bulbs on the stem just below ground.

L. jankae See *L. carniolicum.*

L. japonicum (L) The Japanese 'Bamboo Lily'. The slender stem grows 40–100cm in height with rather scattered, dark green lanceolate leaves up to 20cm long and about 2·5cm wide. The inflorescence is one to five-flowered, the soft-pink trumpet-shaped flowers being about 15cm long and held horizontally. It is stem-rooting. In its natural habitat in Japan it grows at 300–1000m altitude in humus-rich soil in wooded situations. I do not have this lily at present and do not find it very easy to grow. It requires well-drained soil with plenty of leafmould and protection from early frosts if it emerges too early. *L. rubellum* is like a dwarf form of it, growing 40–80cm in height with shorter, broader, leaves and smaller flowers about 6–8cm in length. It is a mountain plant in Japan and is much hardier than *L. japonicum* in Britain.

L. longiflorum (L) The common white trumpet lily which is sold in florists' shops. It grows up to 100cm in height and bears one to five flowers and many scattered shiny deep-green lanceolate leaves about 16–20cm long and 1–5cm wide. The funnel-shaped flowers are pure white, very fragrant and about 15–20cm long with recurved tips to the segments. It is stem-rooting. I have never tried this out of doors in Surrey but it is said to be hardy in some of the milder counties in warm sunny borders. Normally it is grown as a cool greenhouse plant where it will flower in as little as six months from seed. It is native to the Ryukyu Islands at low altitudes in rock pockets.

L. mackliniae A beautiful lily which is difficult to place in any of the sections as accepted here. It is rather closely related to some species of *Nomocharis*. The stem is about 20–80cm in height with numerous scattered, narrowly lanceolate leaves up to 8cm long and 0·5–1cm wide. The one to five flowers are arranged in an umbel and are pendulous, open bell-shaped about 4–5cm long. The colour is white, flushed pinkish-purple on the outside. Although not a large flower, the segments are broad, giving the flowers a substantial appearance. It is stem-rooting. On the Burma–India border area of Manipur it was said by F. Kingdon-Ward to be common on grassy slopes at 2290–2440m. It is not a difficult plant in cultivation, preferring cool positions in leafy or peaty soil which is well drained.

L. martagon The well-known Turk's Cap Lily which grows up to 150cm in height with whorls of dark green oblanceolate leaves up to 15cm long and 6–7cm wide and a raceme of up to 50 pendulous flowers. The segments roll right back until the tips touch the pedicels. In colour it varies a great deal but the most common form is of a dull pinkish purple with darker spots. It is stem-rooting. *L. martagon* is the most widespread lily, occurring in Europe and Asia from Portugal east to

Asia Minor and Russia, as far as the Mongolian border. It normally inhabits woodland and open meadows at altitudes of up to 2500m often on limestone formations. Var. *album* is a beautiful albino which is as easy or easier than the coloured forms. Var. *cattaniae* (var. *dalmaticum*) is a striking form with blackish-wine-coloured flowers. I have seen this in the Velebit mountains of Dalmatia where it occurs in pure colonies with no typical forms in the same population. It breeds true from seed. *L. martagon* and its variants are easily grown in most positions in the garden, although they will not tolerate very deep shade. It is a very suitable species for naturalizing in grass.

L. maximoviczii (M) This is often placed as a variety of the yellow-flowered *L. leichtlinii* which is much more difficult to obtain or to grow. *L. maximoviczii* has slender stems 60–200cm in height which creep underground horizontally before emerging. The numerous leaves are narrowly lanceolate up to 15cm long and about 1cm wide. The pendulous flowers have slender reflexed segments of bright reddish-orange spotted darker purplish-brown. It is a stem-rooting lily, from mountain areas of Japan and Korea and is hardy in Britain. It is best grown in semi-shade in a sandy soil with plenty of leafmould added.

L. nepalense (L) A curious and beautiful lily which is not easy to grow and rather tender in most parts of Britain. The stem creeps horizontally before emerging and often carries bulblets on the underground portion. It is about 70–100cm in height with well-spaced, scattered, lanceolate leaves 10–15cm long and 2–3·5cm wide. The one to three flowers are pendulous, carried on arching pedicels, and are trumpet shaped with the segments recurving at their tips. Each flower is about 15cm long and about the same in diameter across the mouth. The colour is rather extraordinary, a yellowish-green suffused or blotched with purple inside the funnel, although this is lacking in var. *concolor*. It is a stem-rooting lily. *L. nepalense* grows wild in the Himalaya in Nepal, Bhutan and Kumaon at altitudes of 2000–3000m on grassy hill slopes. It is best grown in a cool greenhouse border made up with well-drained loam and leafmould.

L. pardalinum (M) An easily-grown lily for a moist position and suitable for naturalizing in a semi-wild garden. It grows up to 200cm in height, usually with whorls of light green leaves up to 20cm long and 4–5·5cm wide. The flowers are numerous, pendulous on long pedicels, and are shaped like those of a Martagon lily with segments rolled right back to touch the pedicel. The colour is a brilliant orange-red becoming more red towards the tips of the segments and spotted with deep brown-red towards the centre, presumably this having prompted the vernacular name of 'Leopard Lily'. It is not stem-rooting. *L. pardalinum* is a native of California in the coast ranges and in cultivation presents no difficulties. It prefers damp, but not boggy, sites in full sun or dappled shade and when growing well will soon form large clumps because the bulbs are rather rhizome-like and they branch freely. These clumps can be broken up in late summer or early autumn into single bulbs. There are several variants of *L. pardalinum*, sometimes offered by nurserymen.

L. pomponium (M) One of my favourite lilies, although I cannot claim great success with it in cultivation. It is a slender, graceful plant 60–90cm in height with very many linear silver-edged leaves up to 15cm long and only 1cm wide. The four to nine pendulous Turk's Cap flowers have the segments tightly rolled back to touch the long pedicels which are held up at an angle of about 45°. In texture the flowers have a wax-like quality and are brilliant red with black spots in the centre. It is stem-rooting. In the wild it grows on sunny slopes in the Maritime Alps of Italy and France. The best colony I have seen is in the garden of Mrs McConnel in Farnham, Surrey where it is planted at the foot of a large Lawson's cypress on the sunny side so that it gets very hot in summer. It certainly prefers neutral or alkaline soils and good drainage.

L. pyrenaicum (M) A long-cultivated and popular lily very suitable for naturalizing. The 40–120cm stem is densely covered with narrowly lanceolate leaves up to 15cm long and 1·5–2cm wide, and carries up to ten pendulous Turk's Cap flowers of a rather greenish yellow with black spots and lines in the centre. They have a rather disagreeable odour. The anthers are orange-brown and are a rather striking contrast to the yellow segments. It is stem-rooting. Its native habitat is in woods and grassy places in the Pyrenees and northern Spain. Var. *rubrum* has reddish-orange flowers. *L. pyrenaicum* is an easy lily which can be grown in full sun or slight shade in herbaceous borders or a semi-wild garden. I have seen it thriving in grass beneath trees.

L. regale (L) Probably the best known of the white trumpet lilies since it is hardy and easily grown. It has 100–200cm rather wiry stems with numerous alternate, linear, deep-green leaves up to 13cm long and about 0·5cm wide, and one to thirty, 15cm long, scented trumpet-shaped flowers which are white inside with a yellow throat and purplish on the exterior. It is a stem-rooting lily, occurring wild in western China in grassy places and in scrub on mountain slopes and rock crevices. It is tolerant of most types of soil in cultivation but prefers open situations and will not tolerate heavy shade. Although only introduced to Britain in the 1920s by E. H. Wilson, it rapidly became very popular and plentiful for it flowers quickly from seed. Indeed, it was such an easily raised plant that the famous firm of W. A. Constable from Tonbridge Wells offered in their 1938–39 catalogue 'fine flowering bulbs' at the rate of 500 for £7.10.0!

L. speciosum (M) This grows to about 170cm in height with scattered, leathery, deep green leaves up to 20cm long and 5–6cm wide. The normally five to ten (sometimes many more) pendulous flowers are up to 15cm in diameter and have broad overlapping undulate-edged segments which reflex and curl inwards at their tips to nearly touch the pedicels. Towards the centre they have long hair-like protuberances. The colour varies greatly but the most common form is white with crimson-rose suffusion and with darker crimson protuberances near the base of the segments. Variants include pure white (var. *album*) and deep crimson-carmine ('Melpomene') but there are several others with differing amounts of crimson suffusion. *L. speciosum* is a stem-rooting lily. It occurs wild in Japan, Taiwan and China in rocky places in light shade. In cultivation it is not a difficult lily, given a leafmould-rich soil with plenty of grit for drainage.

L. superbum (M) A large, very vigorous lily which will grow 150–250cm in height, with lanceolate leaves in whorls up the stem. The ten to 30 flowers are pendulous with reflexing segments up to 10cm in length, like a large Martagon in shape but the colour is orange becoming reddish towards the tips of the segments and deep purplish-red spotted near the centre. It is stem-rooting and has a curious bulb which travels sideways in the soil by means of a thick stolon. In its natural habitat in the central and eastern United States it is a plant of dampish meadows and marshes. It requires an acid soil with plenty of moisture in the growing season and presents no problems if given a moist sandy loam with plenty of peat or leafmould.

L. szovitsianum (M) A beautiful large-flowered Martagon which is of robust habit, growing up to 150cm in height. The leaves are scattered, lanceolate and hairy on the underside. The raceme carries up to 25 pendulous, 10cm-diameter yellow flowers which have the segments curled back at the tips, although not rolled right in to touch the pedicel as in *L. martagon*. The edges of the segments are usually spotted blackish. It is a stem-rooting lily, growing wild in the southern Caucasus and north-east Turkey amongst shrubs and in light woods. *L. szovitzianum* is a magnificent garden lily in Britain usually presenting no problems in semi-shade in the heavier soils, where it is very long-lived. It prefers a cool site with plenty of moisture in summer and is very suitable for growing in grass. *L. monadelphum* is superficially very similar but has the filaments joined together towards the base and yellow pollen whereas *L. szovitsianum* has free filaments and brown pollen.

L. tigrinum (M) The well-known Tiger Lily which is cheap to buy from nurseries but is often badly infected with virus. It reaches 150cm in height and has scattered linear-lanceolate dark green leaves which have bulbils in their axils. Up to 20 or more pendulous flowers are produced in a raceme and these are about 10cm in diameter, orange-red with blackish-purple spots towards the centre, with the segments reflexed and inrolled at the tips in true *Martagon* style, although the whole flower is much larger. It is a stem-rooting lily, probably wild in China and possibly also in Japan, although it has been cultivated for many centuries and it is difficult to say where it originated. Given a warm site in a lime-free soil, *L. tigrinum* presents no difficulty, although it is very susceptible to virus. Unfortunately it is usually self-sterile, although a self-fertile (diploid) form is known; one must therefore rely on the bulblets for propagation purposes. These, unlike seeds, transmit any virus from the parent plants. There are several varieties of *L. tigrinum* including var. *flaviflorum*, a clear pale yellow with purple spots; var. *splendens* with large flowers and robust growth, similar in colour to the type; a rather ghastly double, var. '*Flore-pleno*', which nevertheless has been in cultivation for at least 100 years and still has its admirers; and var. *fortunei* with many orange-scarlet flowers and generally larger in its general appearance than the typical *L. tigrinum*.

Lycoris Amaryllidaceae

A few of the species in this East Asian genus have been grown in Britain but they have never been as popular as nerines, which they closely resemble. Possibly this is because they are not very free-flowering here and people have despaired. I must admit to being unsuccessful myself, the only flowers which I have seen being from bulbs sent by a friend in Japan, Don Elick. In their first season after arrival these have flowered beautifully, and most handsome plants they are, so I shall strive to keep them going. Mr Elick says that in Japan they tend to grow and flower well along the verges of cultivated fields and that their roots are never dormant so that they may take several years to become well established after planting. The best chance of success seems to be to plant the bulbs in a sunny bed in a cool greenhouse and keep them as hot and dry as possible during the summer months when they are dormant. In milder counties they can be tried at the foot of a south wall in the open, since they will stand a few degrees of frost without damage. Growth begins between July and September in Britain, with luck commencing with a flower stem, then the leaves appear afterwards and remain green until late spring when water should be withheld until the following autumn. If the bulbs, which are like large daffodil bulbs, are to be moved or divided up, this should be carried out just before flowering time. Pot culture can be tried using deep pots and a considerable amount of feeding during the growing season. Some granular slow-release fertilizer which is not too high in nitrogen content seems best and I can say that I get wonderful leaves if nothing else!

Since some of the *Lycoris* species from China are little known, it is difficult to assess exactly how many there are. The estimates vary between eight and 17, all natives of China and Japan. Like other amaryllids of this type, they have a bare flower-stem crowned by an umbel of several flowers and the leaves in a separate basal fan coming up alongside the old inflorescence. Each flower has a short tube and six narrow segments forming a funnel-shaped flower, or recurving somewhat to leave the stamens protruding a long way. There is a small, very insignificant, corona present which is of no importance when trying to distinguish the species. The flowers can be more or less regular in shape or the segments can be arranged unequally, giving an irregular flower. This feature, and the absence or presence of a pale line along the centre of the leaves, constitute the major divisions in the genus.

My information about the species I have not grown has been gleaned from original descriptions, illustrations, herbarium specimens and, in particular, from an article by Hamilton P. Traub in *Plant Life* vol. 13.*

L. albiflora 30–50cm in height. Leaves 1–1·5cm wide, strap-shaped, with a pale line along the centre. Flowers irregular, about 5cm long, creamy-white sometimes tinged pinkish, with segments about 0·5–1cm wide, 3·5–4·5cm long and a tube about 1cm long. It is sterile and is sometimes quoted as being a hybrid of

* American Plant Life Society, La Jolla, California 1957

oomeria crocea, *a yellow-flowered Californian bulb*

lochortus luteus, *a yellow Mariposa lily from California, showing two forms*

The strange Calochortus obispoensis *occurs wild in California*

The showy Calochortus vestae, *a Mariposa lily with creamy red-blotched flowers*

The blue-flowered Camassia quamash, *a tough North American bulb suitable for borders or naturalizing in grass*

Cardiocrinum giganteum *at home in a 'wild garden' setting*

Opposite top   Cypella peruviana, *a beautiful Andean plant requiring a cool greenhouse in most of Britain*

Opposite bottom   The blue Cypella plumbea *requires a warm wall or cool greenhouse in Britain*

Left   Fritillaria acmopetala, *an easily-grown species from the eastern Mediterranean*

Below   Fritillaria imperialis *in its beautiful yellow form*

Above left   A robust plum-coloured form of Fritillaria persica *from southern Turkey*
Above right   Galtonia princeps, growing in a warm border in Surrey
Below   Gladiolus callianthus, formerly Acidanthera bicolor, *has sweetly-scented white flowers*

Iris bucharica, *an easy 'Juno' iris suitable for a sunny border*

Above left Iris cycloglossa, *a very rare 'Juno' iris from Afghanistan, introduced to cultivation by Per Wendelbo*

Above right Iris xiphium *var. 'lusitanica', the yellow Portuguese form of the Spanish iris*

Left Leopoldia comosa, *the tassel hyacinth, with its tuft of sterile flowers above the paler fertile ones*

Lilium auratum, *the golden-rayed lily of Japan. It thrives in cool, well-drained soils such as this north-facing raised bed can provide*

Above left   Lilium bulbiferum, *showing the developing bulbils in the leaf axils*

Above right   Lilium duchartrei, *a stoloniferous species suitable for a woodland garden*

Left   Milla biflora, *a little-known member of the lily family, from Central America*

Opposite top   Nomocharis mairei, *one of the most showy species in cultivation*

Opposite bottom   Nomocharis pardanthina *has pinkish flowers with variable spotting*

Opposite top   A group of Notholirion macrophyllum

Opposite bottom   Close-up of the lily-like Notholirion macrophyllum *which has pale lilac-blue flowers. It grows wild in the Himalaya range*

Left   The showy South African Ornithogalum saundersiae *is best lifted for the winter when grown in Britain*

Below   Pancratium maritimum growing in sand by the sea in Greece

posite top   The Mexican Tigridia bicolor *produces a long succession of flowers in summer*

posite bottom   Tigridia galanthoides, *the 'snowdrop-flowered' Tigridia*

ove   Tigridia vanhouttei: *this is one of the easiest species to grow but has rather dull flowers*

The yellow Triteleia ixioides *occurs wild in California and Oregon*

L. aurea × *L. radiata*. It is said to occur in Japan. I had this in flower for the first time in 1976, and most handsome it is. *L. houdyshelii* also has irregular white flowers and leaves with a stripe. The very undulate segments are about 5cm in length. China.

L. aurea About 40–60cm in height. Leaves roughly 1–1·8cm wide, glaucous, with a paler median stripe, narrowly elliptical or nearly strap-shaped. Flowers irregular, yellow-orange with very undulate segments about 1cm wide and a perianth tube about 1·5cm long. It is probably a widespread species, from China, Japan, the Ryukyus and Formosa. Certainly the Golden Spider Lily is one of the best known in cultivation and is a very attractive species looking extremely like a yellow *Nerine*. *L. traubii* has deep yellow irregular flowers with a 1·9cm long tube and segments 1–1·5cm wide. The strap-like or narrow lanceolate leaves are said to be dark green with a stripe. I have not seen this species. Thought to be from Formosa.

L. caldwellii This is said to be rather an in-between species because it combines two of the major features which are used to divide the genus; it has an irregular flower, but linked with plain green leaves with no stripe. It has pale yellow flowers with the stamens shorter than the segments which are about 7cm long, with a tube about 2–2·5cm long. China.

L. haywardii This has nearly regular funnel-shaped flowers with bluish-tipped purple segments about 4cm long and the tube is slightly more than 1cm long. The leaves are less than 2cm wide and have no paler stripe, and the stamens are held within the flower, not exserted beyond the segments. Japan.

L. incarnata Belongs to the group with regular flowers and no paler stripe in the leaf. Flowers pale pink, quite large, with a tube 1–1·5 cm long. The stamens are not exserted beyond the perianth.

L. koreana This is unknown to me, but is said to have brick red regular flowers with the stamens slightly protruding and a perianth tube about 0·5cm long. The leaves have no paler stripe. Korea.

L. radiata 30–50cm in height. Leaves narrowly strap-shaped, 0·5–1cm wide with a paler central stripe. The irregular red flowers are very spidery-looking with narrow recurving segments and very long protruding stamens. It occurs around fields and in low hills in China, Japan and the Ryukyus. This is one of the hardiest in England and can be tried by a warm wall. There is an orange form on record, and a white form which is probably the same as *L. albiflora*, described above. *L. rosea* is one I have not seen and it sounds similar but with pink flowers and leaves more than 1cm wide. China.

L. sanguinea This grows 30–50cm in height and has 1–1·5cm wide strap-shaped leaves without a paler stripe, but they are a little greyish. Flowers regular bright red or orange-red, 5–6cm long with non-undulate segments and a perianth tube 1–1·5cm long. It occurs on sparsely wooded hills and lower mountain slopes in Japan and China.

L. squamigera This is one of the most well known and can be successfully grown outside in warm areas. My colleague Desmond Meikle has reported good flowering in the autumn of 1976 outside in his Somerset garden, so it obviously enjoys a long hot dry summer rest. It is 50–70cm in height and has strap-shaped unstriped leaves up to 2·5cm wide. The regular funnel-shaped flowers are large, about 9–10cm long, and have non-undulate segments about 1·5cm wide. The tube is 2·5cm or more long and the stamens do not protrude beyond the perianth. The colour is a pale rose-purple tinged with yellow in the throat of the flower. It occurs wild in Japan. This is one of the hardiest and should be tried outside in a warm border where it has protection from cold winds and can be baked in summer. *L. sprengeri* is rather similar in its general features but has smaller flowers, about 7–8cm long, purple-pink, and with a tube less than 1·5cm long. The leaves are up to 2cm wide. Central China. -

L. straminea is not known by me but from its description has straw-coloured irregular flowers with narrow segments, 3·5–4cm long and much-exserted stamens. The tube is about 0·5cm long. It comes from China.

Manfreda Agavaceae

This is related to both *Agave* and *Polianthes*, differing from the former in being bulbous and herbaceous and from the latter in having flowers carried singly on the raceme rather than in pairs as in *Polianthes*. Horticulturally it is not an important genus, few of the species being hardy in Britain, but they can be rather striking when planted out in a warm border, or in a temperate house. Most of the species are from Mexico, but a few reach northwards to the south-east United States. Several of the species have attractively spotted foliage with a bluish-green ground colour. There are about 18 species in all but few are cultivated in Britain, and I do not propose to attempt to describe them all here. The following are perhaps among the best. The genus was reviewed by J. N. Rose in *Contributions from the* US *National Herbarium* 8:15.*

M. longiflora (*Runyonia longiflora*) This was formerly separated as a genus distinct from *Manfreda* because of its sessile anthers and the style being included within the narrow tube, but these characters are of no great significance. It has a rosette of five to seven narrow fleshy basal leaves 10–20cm long which are toothed at the margin. The inflorescence is 30–80cm in height and has a few bract-like leaves and five to 12 stemless, more or less erect brick-red flowers. The tube is very slender, about 3·5cm long, and the spreading lobes 1cm long. It occurs in south-east Texas and northern Mexico. Unfortunately I know this plant only from dried specimens, but the illustration in *Addinsonia* Vol. 7, page 39† shows that it is attractive and worth growing in a cool greenhouse.

M. maculosa (*Agave maculosa*) This has six to ten linear-lanceolate basal leaves which are strongly blotched with brown or dark green and have finely-toothed

* Smithsonian Institution Press, Washington 1903
† New York Botanical Garden 1922

margins. The inflorescence reaches 60cm and has ten to 25 sessile purplish or greenish flowers about 5cm long, with spreading lobes and brown, exserted stamens which are about equal to the perianth tube in length. The tube is more or less straight, as in practically all the *Manfreda* species, and is funnel-shaped. Wild in Texas.

M. singuliflora reaches 60–100cm in height in flower and has eight to ten narrow basal leaves which are rather undulate-edged. The inflorescence has eight to 12 short-pedicelled greenish-purple flowers loosely arranged in a raceme. Each flower is about 3cm long, with a distinct downwards curve in the slender tube, and spreading lobes about 7mm long. It is the only species with a noticeably curved tube. Occurs in Mexico in the hills and mountains near Chihuahua, where it flowers between July and October. One of the most distinct species.

M. variegata A rather handsome plant and possibly hardy, at least in southern Britain. Plants have been raised in recent years from seeds sent by Mrs Sally Walker, collected in Oaxaca State, Mexico at 2600m and these have flowered at Kew in an open sunny border in July. The 2–5cm wide leaves are in a basal rosette, rather blue-green and heavily blotched with deep greenish-purple and the densely-flowered inflorescence rises to about 1–1·5m with deep green flowers and long protruding stamens, much longer than the perianth tube. South-east Texas to Mexico.

Mastigostyla Iridaceae

A small genus of *Tigridia*-like plants from the Andes of South America, little-known in cultivation, but one or two are now grown in specialist collections. Like *Tigridia*, they have short-lived flowers in succession with three large outer segments and three much smaller inner ones. Most of the species have flowers of some shade of lilac or violet. As yet it is too early to say whether they are hardy in Britain, but it is unlikely that they will tolerate any more than cool greenhouse conditions in the colder areas. We can be grateful to Miss Pamela Holt for introducing one recently described species, *M. major*, which is rather attractive. My notes are taken from a plant flowering at Kew, and from the original description.

M. major Grows about 45cm in height with two pleated stem leaves about 1cm wide. The upper leaf is very reduced. Two long narrow green bracts about 8cm long enclose two flowers (up to five according to the description). The outer segments are much larger than the inner and are held out horizontally giving the flower a spread of about 5cm. Basically the colour is mid-blue, the outer segments having white lines towards the base and the inner ones are blue at their tips, becoming yellow at their bases. The scent is rather reminiscent of *Iris unguicularis* or primroses. It grows in Peru at about 3700m but in spite of this altitude will probably require a cool greenhouse in Britain. Like most high-altitude Peruvian bulbs it will probably flower in spring in England, but as yet it has not been cultivated for long enough to be sure of its behaviour.

The other species of *Mastigostyla*, such as *M. hoppii*, are much more dwarf than this species.

Milla Liliaceae

A mainly central American genus from Mexico, Guatemala and southern Arizona known very little in British gardens. Only one species, *M. biflora*, has been cultivated to any extent and even that is rarely seen. It is not hardy in the south-east, but can be grown outside satisfactorily in some gardens of the south-west. Millas have a corm covered with brownish tunics, giving rise to long narrow leaves and a slender leafless stem with an umbellate inflorescence. The flowers are held upright and are either white with green stripes, pinkish or blue. They have a long tube (not a true perianth tube but an extension to the ovary) and six spreading segments, and differ greatly in size from species to species, *M. biflora* and *M. magnifica* being the most striking.

M. biflora This grows up to 40cm in height with very narrow linear leaves and one to seven scented flowers which are white with a long graceful 10–20cm greenish tube. The perianth segments spread out flat to give the flower a diameter of 5–8cm. The segments have a green line running along the centre. It occurs wild in Arizona, Mexico and Guatemala, mainly in volcanic soils at altitudes up to 2600m. *M. biflora* is a beautiful plant and one I would very much like to be able to grow well. Sally Walker once collected some seed of high-altitude plants and these grew well for a while but never reached flowering size. Terry Jones cultivates it very successfully in the south-west and I think it presents little difficulty in the milder areas. It flowers in late summer or autumn both in the wild and in cultivation. *M. bryanii* from Mexico is very similar but has the flowers on 1–5cm pedicels. In *M. biflora* the flowers are sessile. *M. rosea* is probably related to *M. bryanii* with its pedicelled flowers but differs in having a shorter tube, about 5cm long, and is of a pinkish colour.

M. magnifica This grows to about 50cm in height and has more or less cylindrical narrow leaves. The flowers are carried in a dense umbel, sometimes as many as 20 or 30. Each flower is very fragrant, about 5cm in diameter and has a tube about 12cm long. The colour is white with green stripes, as in *M. biflora*, but the rounded leaves and many-flowered inflorescence make it quite distinct. It occurs wild in Mexico and is probably not in cultivation in Britain unfortunately.

Two other species, *M. delicata* and *M. mortoniana*, are known from Guerrero State in Mexico but are not in cultivation. The first has small pinkish flowers and the latter, larger blue flowers about 3cm in diameter.

Moraea Iridaceae

An African genus related to *İris* and superficially rather similar but differing in having fibrous-coated corms and usually flowers with no perianth tube. In *Iris* the six petals normally join into a tube at the base. Otherwise the flowers of *Moraea* are similar in form to those of an *Iris*, with three large outer segments like the 'falls' in Iris, and three inner smaller ones corresponding to the 'standards'. In many cases these are extremely small. The styles are petal-like, also as in *Iris*, and are bilobed and usually similar in colour to the segments.

It is a large genus, but very few are in cultivation in Britain, which is unfortunate because there are many very beautiful species. They can be divided very roughly into (1) tropical African species which are not at all hardy and require a temperate greenhouse in Britain, growing and flowering in summer; (2) eastern Cape ('summer-rainfall') species which are the most useful since they grow in summer, lie dormant in winter and are hardier, at least in southern England; and (3) south-western Cape ('winter-rainfall') species, which although fairly hardy make their growth in winter and flower in early spring and are thus no use out of doors in Britain. These can be grown successfully in a cool greenhouse which is kept just frost-free. Obviously the species which will concern us most in cool temperate areas are the summer-flowering ones from the eastern Cape and one or two of these are quite well known. However, they do not rival the gaudy Peacock Moraeas from the south-west Cape which must have a frost-free house and are kept dry during the summer.

The genus is being revised by Dr Peter Goldblatt who recognizes 26 species from the eastern Cape region. In all, there are probably about 50 or 60 species in Africa.

M. alticola A recently described species, by Peter Goldblatt in 1973. It is similar to *M. spathulata* but is even larger and will undoubtedly be the best of the yellow-flowered species for British gardens. The basal leaf is flat, up to 3cm wide and has a thick margin, but the species is mainly recognized by the 'neck' of pale brownish netted fibres which sheath the leaves and stem some distance above the ground. The flowers are pale yellow with a darker stain in the centre of the falls, and about 8–10cm in diameter. It grows on the top of the Drakensberg Mountains of Natal and Lesotho, up to 3300m altitude. To date it has made sizeable clumps in my garden in a warm but dampish situation. The foliage is evergreen but remains undamaged by frost and it has all the signs of being a first rate garden plant. It flowers in summer.

M. gigandra One of the gaudy Peacock Moraeas and only suitable for greenhouse cultivation. It grows about 40–60cm in height and has large flattish flowers 6–8cm in diameter. The ground colour of the flower is white or lilac with an orange eye in the centre with a blue zone surrounding it. South-west Cape, flowering in early spring in Britain.

M. glaucopsis A Peacock Moraea, growing about 30cm in height and having medium-sized white or bluish flowers with a brilliant blue central eye. Flowers in late spring in Britain. South-west Cape.

M. huttonii Another tall species with large yellow flowers although these are a little smaller than those of *M. spathulata* or *M. alticola*. It grows to about 1m in height with a flat basal leaf. The flowers have a deeper yellow stain and brown markings in the centre of the falls and a brown or purple mark on each of the style branches. It occurs in the eastern Cape and Lesotho and flowers in summer in Britain. Since it grows naturally alongside streams it is best planted in a dampish spot where it gets plenty of sun.

M. moggii A robust species up to 60cm in height with a single very long channelled basal leaf about 1·5cm wide. The green bracts of the inflorescence enclose several very large flowers which are bright yellow in the plant cultivated in Britain (subsp. *moggii*) but can be white (subsp. *albescens*) and are about 6–9cm in diameter. It occurs in moist grassland or rocky hilltops in the eastern Cape and flowers in Britain in late summer where it is a hardy and very useful plant for the herbaceous border or sunny bed by a wall. As far as I know the white subspecies, which is said to be much earlier flowering, is not yet in cultivation.

M. neopavonia (*M. pavonia*) A Peacock Moraea about 30–45cm in height with large 4–5cm diameter flattish flowers with rounded petals. It is naturally very variable and many hybrids exist between this and mainly *M. villosa*, but it is usually yellow or orange with a blue zone around a heavily spotted central eye. Flowering in early spring in Britain. South-west Cape.

M. polystachya This attractive species grows up to 50cm in height in cultivation with several long, 1–2cm wide, channelled leaves which are rather untidy when fully grown. The inflorescence is about 5cm in length, consisting of several greenish or papery-brown bracts enclosing a long succession of large flowers, which are clear lilac-blue with a bright yellow spot in the centre of each of the 'falls' and about 5–6cm in diameter. It is widespread in southern Africa from the southern Cape north to south-west Africa (Namibia) and Malawi in a wide variety of situations from dry rocky ground to grassy places. I have two different forms of this species, one which grows and flowers in late winter and the other in late summer or autumn. This is probably accounted for by its wide distribution, the conditions in, for example, south-west Africa and Malawi being very different. One of my plants was collected in the latter country. Both forms increase very well by seed and corm division and I shall try some outside. In mild areas such as the south and west of England and the southern United States the winter-flowering form is very useful and I have seen it flowering in January outdoors in California.

M. spathulata (*M. spathacea*) A clump-forming species, each corm with a single long, often grey-green, narrow flattish basal leaf. Stems reaching 1m high with a several-flowered inflorescence. Each flower is 6–8cm in diameter and bright yellow, sometimes with darker markings in the centre of the falls. It is a very variable species and four subspecies are recognized. Even within subsp. *spathulata*, the one in cultivation in Britain, there is considerable variation and it may be worth growing several different forms. It flowers in early to mid-summer in southern England and is one of the best known of the Moraeas in cultivation, requiring a warm sunny border. *M. spathulata* occurs in the southern and eastern

Cape in grassy places at varying altitudes from 30–3000m. It is very similar to *M. moggii*, differing mainly in being clump-forming.

M. villosa This is another Peacock Moraea, related to *M. pavonia* and hybridizing with it. It has very hairy leaves and the slender flower stems reach 35–50cm in height. The flattish rounded flowers are 5–6cm in diameter and are usually mauve or purple with a vivid blue or greenish eye. It flowers in late spring in Britain. South-west Cape, in stony places up to 700m altitude.

Narcissus Amaryllidaceae

The daffodils and narcissi, of course, form a subject all of their own and books have been, and will continue to be, written about them. I do not propose therefore to delve deeply into the history of their cultivation and hybridization for it is the wild species which interest me, although I acknowledge the beauty and garden worthiness of the many cultivars available. To deal with 400 years of cultivation, selection and breeding in the space I have available would be impossible and would to some extent duplicate the information available in books such as E. A. Bowles's *A Handbook of Narcissus* (Martin Hopkinson, 1934) and Fernandes's work on *Narcissus* published in RHS *Daffodil and Tulip Year Book, 1968*. Additionally, I am confining myself to the taller species, so the number of wild species left for me to deal with is very limited. A few long-established hybrids have become stabilized and form apparently wild populations and I have included these in the alphabetical sequence.

N. alpestris See under *N. pseudonarcissus*.

N. bertolonii See under *N. tazetta*.

N. bicolor This belongs to the Pseudonarcissus section, or trumpet daffodils. It has solitary flowers carried horizontally on a stem up to 40cm in height. They are, as the name suggests, bicoloured, with the perianth segments pale yellow or cream and the corona deep yellow. The corona is more or less cylindrical and with only slight crinkling around its rim, about 3·5–4cm long. The name has been given to a wide range of garden forms but there is however a wild representative, *N. abscissus*, which occurs in the Pyrenees. This is very distinctive, with its nearly straight corona which almost looks as if it has been trimmed off with scissors with practically no 'flaring' at the mouth.

N. × biflorus (*N. × medioluteus*) (*N. poeticus × N. tazetta*) This usually has two flattish flowers on a 30–60cm stem, with white perianth segments and a shallow yellow cup about 1cm across. There are now a great many hybrids of this parentage, but the cross seems to be established in the wild in southern France. It is rather intermediate, as one might expect, with its long tube (from *N. poeticus*), yellow corona (from *N. tazetta*) and two flowers (one in *N. poeticus* and three or more in *N. tazetta*).

N. canaliculatus See under *N. tazetta*.

N. canariensis See under *N. tazetta*.

N. corcyrensis See under *N. tazetta.*

N. cypri See under *N. tazetta.*

N. × *dubius* (*N. papyraceus* × *N. requienii*) This resembles *N. papyraceus* in most of its features but has very narrow greyish leaves, this reduced leaf width presumably being derived from the rather dwarf *N. requienii*, which is not dealt with here. The creamy-white flowers are about 1–1·5cm in diameter and up to five or six in an umbel. It occurs wild in north-east Spain and southern France in rocky places. I have not cultivated this but it is said to grow best in a frame where it can be sun-baked in summer.

N. elegans One of the few autumn-flowering species, having slender leaves at flowering time, up to 6mm wide. The smallish flowers are carried on a 10–35cm stem in an umbel of usually three to seven and are white and sweetly scented. The lanceolate, pointed, perianth segments reflex a little giving slight prominence to the very shallow greenish cup which is only 3–4cm in diameter. It occurs wild in southern Italy and Sicily. Although similar to the more widespread *N. serotinus*, it can be distinguished by the more numerous flowers and wider leaves which are visible at flowering time. Flowering September to October. It occurs in southern Italy and Sicily and North Africa where it grows in dryish grassy or scrubby places up to 500m. Unfortunately this is very rare in cultivation.

N. hispanicus See under *N. pseudonarcissus.*

N. × *incomparabilis* A well-known bicoloured *N. poeticus* × *N.* × *pseudonarcissus* hybrid which probably occurs naturally in southern France. It is up to 45cm in height with solitary slightly fragrant flowers having an undulate funnel-shaped orange or yellow corona 1–2·5cm long and 2–2·5cm across at the mouth and pale yellow or cream perianth segments, not at all reflexed. The name 'incomparabilis' has been given to a division of the genus, covering many and varied hybrids. They have also been separated by some botanists as the genus *Queltia*, after Nicholas de Quelt who recorded the hybrid near Luchon. There are now numerous single and double varieties which may have arisen from these two parents.

N. italicus See under *N. tazetta.*

N. × *intermedius* A dark-green leaved *N. jonquilla* hybrid, probably with *N. tazetta* as the other parent, growing about 30–40cm in height with three to ten long-tubed sweetly scented flowers of a bright yellow. The shallow wavy-margined corona is about 3–5mm deep, slightly darker yellow, and the perianth segments are not reflexed at all. A well-known and attractive plant in cultivation and occurring as a natural hybrid in the Pyrenees. It really differs very little from *N. jonquilla* but the leaves are wider, usually 0·5–1cm wide, and the perianth tube is 1·5–2cm long.

N. jonquilla The well-known smallish-flowered jonquil which is so popular for its fragrance. The leaves are deep green and rather long and narrow, usually 3–5mm wide. The two to five bright yellow flowers are about 2–3cm in diameter and have a 2–3cm long straight tube. The corona is undulate and about 3–5mm

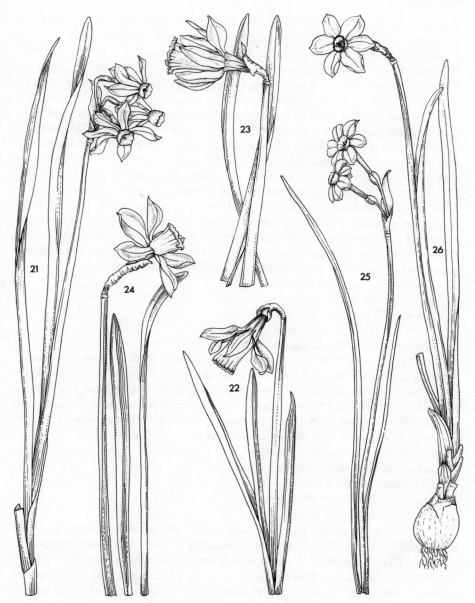

21 *Narcissus tazetta*
22 *Narcissus alpestris*
23 *Narcissus pseudonarcissus*

24 *Narcissus incomparabilis*
25 *Narcissus jonquilla*
26 *Narcissus poeticus*

deep and the segments are not reflexed. It occurs wild in Spain and Portugal in moist grassy places. In gardens it needs a warm sunny spot.

N. lobularis See *N. obvallaris*, under *N. pseudonarcissus*.

N. longispathus A rather uncommon species in cultivation, belonging to the Pseudonarcissus group. It is a very robust plant reaching 150cm in height, although in cultivation it is much smaller. The grey 1–1·5cm wide leaves are usually about 50cm long. The most noticeable feature of the inflorescence is the very long spathe, usually 6–10cm, and a long pedicel, 4–10cm long. The normally solitary flower is yellow with a slightly darker yellow corona 2·5–3cm long and is very like that of *N. pseudonarcissus*. It apparently occurs only in the Cazorla area of south-east Spain where it grows alongside streams at 1300–1500m. C. Stocken grew this in Devon near a pool where it was very vigorous and produed up to three flowers in an umbel. I do not possess this at present but I remember growing it at Wisley some 15 years ago from a collection made by Heywood and Davis. At first it was grown in a pot which was obviously wrong, taking the habitat into consideration, so it was then planted out in the damp lower part of the alpine meadow but it did not thrive for long.

N. × medioluteus See *N. × biflorus*.

N. moschatus See under *N. pseudonarcissus*.

N. nevadensis See under *N. pseudonarcissus*.

N. nobilis See under *N. pseudonarcissus*.

N. obvallaris See under *N. pseudonarcissus*.

N. × odorus This is a hybrid between *N. jonquilla* and *N. pseudonarcissus*, growing up to 40cm in height with long slender green leaves. The 5cm diameter bright yellow, scented flowers vary in number from one to four and have a straight perianth tube about 2cm long. The corona is widely funnel-shaped and 1·5–2cm deep. An attractive plant combining the deep yellow flowers and green leaves of *N. jonquilla* with the longer corona of *N. pseudonarcissus*.

N. pachybolbus See under *N. tazetta*.

N. pallidiflorus See under *N. pseudonarcissus*.

N. panizzianus See under *N. tazetta*.

N. papyraceus See under *N. tazetta*.

N. patulus See under *N. tazetta*.

N. poeticus The Pheasant's Eye Narcissus. A very well-known species in gardens, for it usually flowers after all the other species have ended. It is a variable species, from 25–45cm in height with grey leaves usually slightly shorter than the inflorescence. The solitary flowers are very flat in appearance, about 3·5–6cm in diameter with a very shallow crinkled corona only 1–3mm deep, of a dark yellow or reddish colour. Occurs wild in southern Europe from Spain eastwards to Greece, in moist or wet alpine meadows. The great range of variation has resulted in several species having been described, but they obviously overlap in their features and all belong to *N. poeticus*. Thus the name *N. radiiflorus* has no real standing, since it applies to a local form from the Balkans which in general has non-overlapping perianth segments and a very small corona. It is perhaps best treated as a variety or subspecies of *N. poeticus*.

N. poeticus is a beautiful plant for naturalizing in damp grassy places such as old orchards. My experience with the true wild plant is that it is not an easy species to grow and should be planted in a damp place but with plenty of sun.

N. polyanthus See under *N. tazetta*.

N. portensis See under *N. pseudonarcissus*.

N. pseudonarcissus A very variable species of trumpet daffodil with a wide distribution, including Britain where it is known as the Lent Lily. Probably there is no really satisfactory classification since the variants overlap in their characters whether they are treated as species, subspecies or forms. To lump them all under one name would be too drastic, and yet to recognize a large number of species would be equally unsatisfactory. The best one can do is to have names for some of the more distinct entities within the group, while accepting that they vary and may overlap in their features. *N. pseudonarcissus* and its relatives have grey leaves (except *N. nevadensis*) and usually grow from 10–70cm in height with leaves slightly shorter than or equalling the flower stem. The flower is usually solitary, either white, yellow or bicoloured and has a long, more or less straight-sided trumpet or corona which may be rather flared at the mouth and crinkled or rather smooth. *N. pseudonarcissus* itself varies from cream to yellow with a usually deeper yellow corona which is not very noticeably expanded at the mouth. It occurs in most of Western Europe from Spain to Germany and north to Britain and is a plant of grassy places or light woodland. *N. pallidiflorus* from the Pyrenees is very similar but has a rather expanded mouth to the corona. *N. nobilis* is bicoloured with the perianth pale and the flared trumpet deep yellow, differing mainly from *N. pseudonarcissus* in having a longer pedicel, usually about 1–2cm long, and the flower often facing horizontally or slightly upwards instead of pendulous. It occurs in northern Spain and northern Portugal and is a fine garden plant for a dampish position. My own plants were brought from Spain by Dick Brummitt and Arthur Chater who rescued them from a valley scheduled for flooding. They grew, apparently in thousands, in what will now be a lake bed. *N. nevadensis* is distinguished by having green rather than grey leaves and more than one flower in the inflorescence. It is a bicoloured form with smallish flowers, the trumpet only 1·5–2·5cm long and scarcely flared at the apex. The plant is restricted to the Sierra Nevada Mountains in southern Spain. *N. obvallaris* (*N. lobularis*), the Tenby Daffodil, is similar to *N. pseudonarcissus* but is more or less uniform in colour and holds its flowers up more so that they are less drooping. Its origin is uncertain and it is naturalized in Wales.

N. portensis is very similar to *N. obvallaris* in having more or less horizontal flowers of uniform yellow, but has a trumpet which becomes wider from base to apex, being 2–4cm wide at the mouth. It occurs in north-west Spain and northern Portugal. Two very distinct variants are *N. alpestris* and *N. moschatus*. They are very similar to each other, having drooping white flowers with the perianth segments lying alongside the trumpet, so that the whole flower has a 'wilted' appearance. *N. moschatus* has the corona slightly flared and is a rather creamy white, while *N. alpestris* has pure white flowers with a straight-sided unflared corona. Both probably occur in the Pyrenees although the origin of the plant cultivated as *N. moschatus* is rather uncertain. They both do fairly well in my garden in a dampish spot among heathers in a sandy soil. My bulbs of *N. alpestris* were given to me by C. Sipkes, collected in the Pyrenees, and these have increased well, although neither of the two drooping white narcissi is very vigorous.

N. hispanicus is one of the largest in this group, with stems up to 70cm in height, or sometimes more. The flowers are usually uniform in colour, horizontal or held slightly upwards, with rather twisted perianth segments. It occurs in south-west France, Spain and Portugal.

N. radiiflorus See under *N. tazetta*.

N. serotinus The most common of the autumn-flowering species, usually producing its flower stems without any leaves present. Young or non-flowering plants have several thread-like leaves. The inflorescence reaches 25cm in vigorous specimens and usually carries one, rarely two, scented white 2–2·5cm diameter flowers which have a very shallow yellow cup. It is very widely distributed around the Mediterranean at low altitudes in maquis or in sandy places. To succeed in cultivation the bulbs need a thorough baking in summer and should be kept frost-free in winter. It flowers in October and November.

N. tazetta The most widespread of all the *Narcissus* species from Spain eastwards to Japan, although whether it is native in many countries is open to considerable doubt. It is extremely variable and has been cultivated for such a long time that there are now many forms, sometimes appearing to be wild but undoubtedly left-overs or escapes from gardens. For example, double forms can be found in parts of southern Greece. *N. tazetta* is a cluster-headed species with up to 20 smallish, very sweetly scented 2–5cm flowers on stems up to 50cm in height. The cup is small, usually only 4–5mm deep and 5–10mm in diameter. There are several related species, some of them best regarded as subspecies of *N. tazetta*, mainly distinguished by flower colour. The flowering time varies widely from late autumn to spring and I have seen forms in the Pelopponese in flower in October.

The commonest and most widespread form of *N. tazetta* has white perianth segments and a deep yellow corona. *N. aureus* from southern France and northern Italy differs only in having large (4–5cm diameter), wholly yellow flowers, the cup sometimes a little darker than the perianth segments. *N. tazetta* subsp. *lacticolor* is perhaps the same as *N. italicus* and is halfway between the 'common' *N. tazetta* and *N. aureus* with creamy-yellow segments and deep yellow corona. It occurs in southern France, Italy and the adjacent islands. *N. bertolonii* has wholly yellow flowers or the cup darker than the pale yellow segments and seems to differ very little from forms of *N. aureus*. The perianth segments are said to be shorter than the perianth tube, whereas in *N. aureus* they equal it. *N. patulus* from southern France, Italy, adjacent islands and parts of the southern Balkans is a dwarf plant with almost prostrate leaves and small flowers, usually about 2cm in diameter. The colour is the same as 'typical' *N. tazetta*. Similar to this is *N. canaliculatus* which can also be regarded as a dwarf form of *N. tazetta*. *N. cypri* is a large and vigorous plant with flowers 4–5cm in diameter, of a similar colour to *N. tazetta*. It is native in Cyprus and Syria. *N. corcyrensis* is a little-known species from north-west Greece, said to have very narrow non-overlapping white perianth segments and a yellow or orange cup.

The white forms of these bunch-flowered narcissi are equally variable and the well known 'paper-white' is an average example of the various members of this group. *N. papyraceus* occurs around the central and western Mediterranean and has flowers about 3–4cm in diameter, up to 20 in each umbel and of a pure glistening white. It is about the most vigorous of the group. *N. panizzianus* has smaller flowers, about 2–2·5cm in diameter, while *N. polyanthus* has greenish instead of grey leaves. *N. canariensis* is a rather tender one from the Canary Islands and was grown beautifully by Eliot Hodgkin in a deep pot in an alpine house. It has flowers only 1–2cm in diameter with rather narrow pointed segments. *N. pachybolbus* is like this but with broader, less acute segments, and inhabits Morocco and Algeria.

I find that all the *N. tazetta* group respond well if given sun-baked conditions but after a dull summer, flowering is often very poor.

N. viridiflorus This is really a botanical curiosity, for it is not hardy nor very showy. It is autumn-flowering, reaching about 25cm in height or sometimes up to 40cm. Up to six scented, bright green flowers 1·5–3cm in diameter are produced, with narrow perianth segments and a very small six-lobed corona. The flowers appear before the leaves. It occurs wild in the western Mediterranean region at low altitudes, flowering in October to November. The best chance of successful cultivation seems to be in a cool greenhouse with a good baking for the bulbs during the summer.

Nectaroscordum Liliaceae

A small genus of bulbous plants closely related to *Allium* and regarded only as a section or subgenus by some botanists. In one of the largest and most recent revisions of *Allium*, Wendelbo in *Flora Iranica*,* treats *Nectaroscordum* as a separate genus. There are about four species, only two of which are in general cultivation. These are easily grown in almost any situation and look well naturalized in grass. They should not be planted in a bulb frame as they can become very invasive.

* 'Alliaceae' (1976), ed. K. H. Rechinger. Akademische Druck u. verlagsanstalt, Graz

Nectaroscordum differs from *Allium* in having the perianth segments 3–7 nerved (1-nerved in *Allium*), an ovary with numerous ovules (few in *Allium*) and the pedicels markedly swollen at the apex.

N. bulgaricum This reaches up to 90cm in height, with large loose umbels of pendulous flowers on long pedicels, becoming erect in the fruiting stage. Leaves basal, deeply channelled and with a very sharply-angled keel. Flowers produced in May or June, bell-shaped and rather like small fritillaries, 1·5–2·5cm long, 2cm wide, whitish or straw-coloured tinged with green. The dried inflorescences make very good winter decorations and are scentless, whereas the fresh plant has a most unpleasant, very strong, garlic-like odour. Wild in Bulgaria and western Turkey.

N. siculum (*N. dioscoridis*) This species is very similar to the last and differs mainly in having green flowers strongly flushed with purple and edged with white. One seedling which has occurred in my garden recently has almost wholly reddish-purple flowers and is worth perpetuating. *N. siculum* is wild in southern France, Sicily, Italy and Sardinia.

N. tripedale This species is not known to be in cultivation unfortunately. It is similar to the others but has smaller flowers 1·2–1·5cm long which are white with about three reddish veins along each segment. It is a native of northern Iraq, south-east Turkey and western Iran.

Nerine Amaryllidaceae

Although there are quite a number of species in this genus – which comes from South Africa and southern tropical Africa – only one is hardy in Britain. They are mostly pinkish in colour and have umbels of flowers which have six narrow perianth segments, often rather undulate. The inflorescence is produced in the autumn before the leaves develop.

Nerines are mostly cultivated as cool greenhouse plants where they are best grown in pots and only re-potted when they become too crowded. Re-potting is carried out in the late summer or early autumn before the inflorescences appear, and in the years when they are not disturbed it is best to feed them through the growing season with a general liquid fertilizer. *N. bowdenii* is completely hardy and requires a sunny border at the foot of a south wall in well-drained soil. I have seen it growing and flowering outside in Britain as far north as Inverness-shire. If the bulbs become too crowded they can be lifted and re-planted with better spacing, but on the whole they are best left undisturbed. Although it is often said that they should be planted near the surface, the bulbs of *N. bowdenii* are best if covered by at least 6cm of soil to give them protection in winter. I once lost quite a lot of bulbs which had become congested and pushed to the surface during a wet, freezing spell in winter.

N. bowdenii This grows up to 70cm in height when in flower with three to nine pale pink flowers in a loose umbel about 15cm in diameter. The narrow perianth segments have wavy edges and curl back somewhat. Although the leaves are produced in late autumn and last through the winter they are very frost-hardy and remain undamaged. In Britain it flowers in September–November. It is a native of the south-west Cape region, often flowering very well after a fire on the grassy or scrub-covered slopes where it grows.

Nomocharis Liliaceae

A genus of about eight species, all extremely beautiful and closely related to *Lilium*, although at times some have also been referred to the genus *Fritillaria*. The whole genus is confined mainly to Tibet and western China and of the known species probably only about four are now in cultivation in Britain, and these are rare. The first introductions of living material were made about 60 years ago, although the genus was first recognized as a new one in 1889. Most of the introductions were made by those great collectors of the early twentieth century, Forrest, Farrer and Kingdon-Ward, and undoubtedly some of the material still in cultivation is derived from these sources. Were it not for the damper climate of Scotland and the skill of the gardeners who handled these gorgeous plants, we would certainly be without them today in Britain, for they do not thrive in relatively dry warm gardens and can really only be regarded as temporary thrills for those in the south.

The bulbs of *Nomocharis* are very similar to those of *Lilium*, but the flowers are flattish and drooping or horizontal with more or less crested or swollen areas at the base of the inner perianth segments. The genus is divided into two, one group having filaments tapering fairly gradually from base to apex and perianth segments with slightly swollen but not crested bases (*N. aperta* and *N. saluenensis*) and the other group having inflated bases to the filaments and perianth segments with crests at the base (*N. pardanthina, N. meleagrina, N. mairei, N. basilissa* and *N. farreri*). *N. synaptica* falls between the two groups with filaments of the former group and segments like the latter group.

In cultivation they require cool conditions with plenty of moisture during the late spring and summer. In Scotland they can be grown in open situations but in the south, cool peaty conditions in semi-shade suit them best. The stems root out just above the bulbs, as do many Lilies, and care must be taken to keep these roots covered with soil. There is no difficulty in raising them from seed and on the occasions when I have been successful it is as a result of sowing them thinly in pots and then in their second year planting the whole pot-ball out into its final position. They will usually flower in about their fourth year from sowing time. All species flower in June or July. Hybrids between the species have occurred in cultivation, making positive identification difficult. The following species are now referred to the genus *Lilium*: *N. euxantha, N. georgei, N. henrici, N. lophophora, N. nana, N. souliei*, since they obviously have greater affinities with that genus than *Nomocharis*.

N. aperta Usually about 60–90cm in height with pairs of opposite lanceolate leaves (they are whorled in the related *N. pardanthina*) in the middle, and solitary leaves in the lower and upper parts of the stem. The nodding 8–10cm diameter flowers, up to six in number, are carried on long horizontal or slightly decurved pedicels and are like flat saucers when fully open. The colour is pale pink blotched with deep reddish-purple towards the base, and the centre has a dark blotch around the nectary. White forms without spots have been recorded in the wild. China, in south-west Szechuan and north-west Yunnan up to 4300m altitude.

N. basilissa This sounds a most gorgeous plant but is little known and probably not now in cultivation. Farrer, the collector, compared its colour to that of Oriental poppies, a bright salmon scarlet without spots. Burma and Yunnan, up to 4300m altitude.

N. farreri See *N. pardanthina*.

N. mairei This grows about 60–70cm in height with whorls of three to six lanceolate leaves, each up to 10cm long. The nodding flowers are flattish, up to 10cm in diameter, and are held on horizontal pedicels. The inner and outer perianth segments differ from each other, the inner being heavily fringed along the edges and narrower than the broad unfringed outer segments. The colour is white, heavily spotted with reddish-purple and with a deep red-purple eye around the nectaries. Two variants are known: (1) var. *leucantha* has larger flowers, very heavily spotted on a white ground and with the top half of the inflated portion of the filament yellow and the basal half purple (in typical *N. mairei* the whole inflated portion is purple); (2) var. *candida* has white flowers completely unspotted except for the central purple gland zone. China in Yunnan in meadows up to 3300m. *N. mairei* is one of the better known, and the most spectacular, species in cultivation.

N. meleagrina Not a well-known species and probably not in cultivation at present. It has several nodding flat flowers, about 10cm in diameter, coloured rose, blotched over the whole surface with red-purple and with all the segments more or less equal in size. The inner segments are fimbriate at their edges but much less so than in *N. mairei*. In the centre of the flower is a strong brownish-red blotch nearly 1cm in diameter. *N. meleagrina* might also be confused with *N. pardanthina*, but *N. meleagrina* has the spotting over the entire flower and more or less equal segments. China, in north-west Yunnan, western Szechuan and in south-east Tibet, at altitudes of 3700 to 4300m.

N. pardanthina One of the better-known species in cultivation, this has been in Britain since about 1914. It grows up to 90cm in height, with whorls of three to six leaves, with one to ten flat drooping flowers with a pink ground colour. The outer segments are slightly smaller than the inner, not fimbriate and not, or only slightly, spotted. The larger, more rounded inner segments are fimbriate and are heavily spotted towards the base, not all over both sets of segments as in *N. meleagrina*, but it also has the dark glandular 'eye' in the centre of the flower. The basal spotting also helps to distinguish this from the heavily spotted *N.*

mairei. China, western Yunnan at about 3000m. *N. farreri* is often referred to as a variety of *N. pardanthina* and is usually more robust, with narrower leaves, and the whitish flowers have only slight fimbriations at the margins, or none at all. The leaves of *N. pardanthina* are about 1·3–2cm wide and 5cm long, while those of *N. farreri* are not more than 1·3cm wide and up to 10cm long. It occurs in Upper Burma at altitudes of up to 4000m and was first collected there by Farrer in 1919.

N. saluenensis Another well-known species in cultivation and not too difficult in southern gardens. Grows up to 90cm in height with leaves in pairs or, rarely, threes and one to six flowers about 9cm in diameter and rather more saucer-shaped than flat. They vary a great deal in colour from white to rose or pale yellow and are usually spotted purple near the base of the segments, which are not fimbriate at the edges. The inner segments are slightly shorter and broader than the outer and have a dark red-purple blotch where the basal nectary is situated. China, in north-west Yunnan, western Szechuan, south-east Tibet and northern Burma, up to 4300m altitude.

N. synaptica Although collected in 1928 by Kingdon-Ward, this was not described as a new species until 1950 when Mr J. R. Sealy made a study of some *Nomocharis* and *Lilium* species. It has white or pinkish flowers heavily purple-blotched and therefore is similar in general appearance to several other species. However, it is said to have low crests at the base of the inner segments but has filaments which taper gradually from base to apex. It thus falls midway between the two basic groups of species. It comes from Assam, in the Delei Valley at 3300–4000m altitude and has probably never been in cultivation.

Notholirion Liliaceae

A genus of only a few species, related to *Lilium* and *Fritillaria*, having features of both. It differs from them in having a few-scaled bulb which is covered in a ribbed tunic and which dies after flowering. The life of the plant is continued by bulblets produced around the base of the dying parent bulb. *Cardiocrinum* is the only other genus in this group to have a bulb which is monocarpic, as this habit is called, but in this case the bulb is not covered by a tunic. The several long narrow basal leaves which are produced in autumn or winter further serve to distinguish the genus, and the very definitely three-lobed style sets it apart from *Lilium, Cardiocrinum* and *Nomocharis*. The flowers are funnel-shaped and in some species widely flared.

In cultivation they have not become very popular since in districts where hard frosts occur the leaves may be damaged. However, if planted where they have protection from shrubs, or in a cold frame covered by a light in winter, they can be satisfactorily grown. The summer treatment should be similar to that given to Nomocharis or Lilies, that is, a cool position with leafmould or peat, but with good drainage. They can be grown fairly easily in pots in a cold or cool greenhouse. One of the best plantings I have ever seen of *Notholirion* was a large raised bed at Highdown, packed with bulbs from end to end. It was not covered in winter, but this Sussex garden is of course very mild and the overwintering leaves were undamaged most years. Propagation is simply by growing on the plentiful bulblets which arise around the parent bulb.

N. bulbuliferum (*N. hyacinthinum*) One of the better-known species and more easily grown than the others, although it does tend to be too prolific, with off-spring which are difficult to grow on to flowering size. Usually about 60–90cm high when in flower, with scattered stem leaves and linear, very long, trailing basal leaves. The ten to 30 horizontal flowers are carried in a loose raceme, on short pedicels, and are funnel-shaped at the base. The six segments flare outwards so that the flower is wide open with the stamens and style somewhat prominently displayed. The colour is pale lilac shading to green on the tips of the segments. Flowers July–August in Britain. Widespread in western China, west to Nepal and in Bhutan, Burma and Sikkim in alpine meadows at about 3000–4500m.

N. campanulatum A beautiful species which I have not grown. It is similar in habit to *N. bulbuliferum* but differs in its flowers, which are drooping bells of deep crimson tipped with green, 4–5cm long. Flowering June–July. Yunnan, Tibet and northern Burma in alpine meadows at 3000–4000m. This is a very rare plant in cultivation and reports of it succeeding are few and far between. It appears to prefer relatively mild damp climates, such as the south-west corner of Scotland offers.

N. koeiei A little-known species and one which possesses several unusual features. It is said to be 50–70cm in height with about 12 leaves scattered up the stem, the lowest 20–30cm long and about 1cm wide. The inflorescence is a dense raceme with 20 to 30 suberect flowers each 4–4·5 cm long, pinkish-purple, funnel-shaped with the tips of the segments flaring outwards, but not recurved. The anthers are yellow. It was collected in western Iran in the province of Luristan at about 1000m altitude. All the other species are essentially Himalayan, whereas this species occurs about 2500km westwards of any other *Notholirion*. It is therefore in a region which experiences hot dry summers and would presumably be best grown with other Middle East bulbs rather than in a cool damp atmosphere. I do not know of it in cultivation.

N. macrophyllum This is the shortest of the species, being only 30–40cm in height when in flower. The basal leaves are bright green, up to 1·5cm wide and about 30cm long in flowering specimens. There are a few narrower stem leaves becoming progressively more bract-like up the stem with the upper ones having flowers in their axils. There are usually only a few flowers, five or six being the maximum. Each flower is a wide open funnel, about 3–4cm long and 5cm across at the mouth, horizontal or slightly pendulous, and is pale lavender spotted purple inside, in two definite zones. The segments are not tipped green. The nectaries can be seen glistening with a drop of liquid, right at the base of the segments, as in many fritillaries. The anthers are purplish with brown-yellow pollen. Flowering May–June in Britain. Wild in Nepal, southern Tibet, Bhutan and Sikkim from 2500–4000m in alpine meadows. My own plants were grown from seed collected by Brian Halliwell in Nepal and they flowered after about four years in a pot kept in a frost-free greenhouse. I have not yet tried them outside for the species is said to be rather tender.

N. thompsonianum Perhaps the best-known species in Britain. It has long trailing basal leaves produced in autumn, followed in spring or early summer by leafy flower-stems up to 90cm in height. The inflorescence is quite dense with a raceme of about ten to 25 more or less horizontal flowers. These are pale rosy-lilac, sweetly scented, about 6·5cm long, funnel shaped with strongly recurving tips to the segments, and protruding stamens. It occurs wild in the western Himalayas from Kumaon west to Kashmir and Afghanistan in sunny dryish places at 1000–2000m. Possibly this species requires more drying out when dormant than the others, so it is best to try it in a warm sunny place with very good drainage.

Ornithogalum Liliaceae

The 'Star of Bethlehem' belongs to a large genus of about 150 species, mainly occurring in north and south temperate regions of the Old World, especially in the Mediterranean, western Asia and in South Africa, although a few dull greenish-flowered species occur in tropical Africa. The only tall species of value in British gardens are a few northern hemisphere ones which are hardy, and even fewer South African ones which can be planted out in spring and lifted for the winter to be stored in a frost-free shed. Most species are easy to grow, producing plenty of seed which takes only three or four years to produce flowering-sized bulbs. Most species have starry white flowers with a green stripe running along the centre of each of the six equal perianth segments, but a few are wholly white or yellow. They are carried in a raceme, which in the dwarf species is reduced so that the flowers appear to be in a head in the centre of the rosette of leaves. All species have basal leaves which in the larger species are usually long and linear and often more or less dying away by flowering time so that the plants look rather untidy. It is better therefore to plant these behind a low evergreen plant so that only the inflorescences show up. Most of the species require a sunny position in well-drained soil, *O. nutans* being a notable exception in being a woodland plant and suitable for naturalizing. All are late spring or early summer flowering unless stated otherwise.

O. arabicum A spectacular species, looking quite different from the majority of northern hemisphere *Ornithogalums*. It can reach about 75cm in height with several 1–3cm wide lanceolate leaves which are short enough to make a 'tidy' rosette, unlike many of the larger species in which they are long and straggling. The large white flowers are flattish, about 4–7cm in diameter, and have a blackish ovary which is a very striking feature of the plant, contrasting well with the

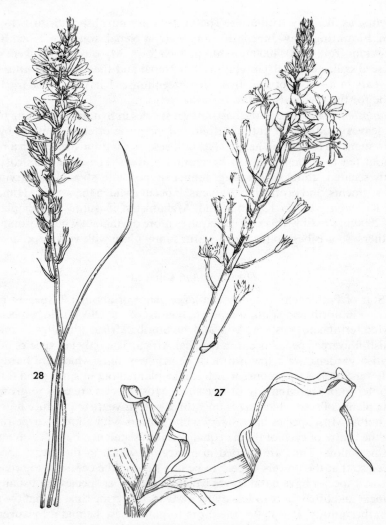

27 *Ornithogalum arcuatum*
28 *Ornithogalum narbonense*

perianth and the large yellow stamens. The inflorescence is a raceme but appears flat-topped because of the lowest flowers being held on long pedicels, almost level with the upper flowers. It is probably wild in several Mediterranean countries, but is difficult to say in which it is native for it is a popular garden plant which naturalizes in suitable climates. I have never grown it very satisfactorily. It requires very hot sunny places or bulb-frame cultivation, as it is a low-altitude plant and must be thoroughly baked in the summer. It flowers in May and June.

O. arcuatum A rather attractive species with a long loose raceme of flowers reaching to about 60cm in height. The leaves are beginning to die away by flowering time so that it is best to plant it behind some other low-growing plant to hide the tatty lower half. The flowers are very pure white with a pale green stripe on each segment and are about 2cm in diameter. Each is carried on a long pedicel, 2–3cm long at the flowering stage but elongating and arching upwards before the flowers are over. It is a native of Iran in fields and dryish stony places. It flowers in May or June in Britain. I have found this a most satisfactory hardy species for growing in an open sunny border where it has increased well from self-sown seedlings. My original plants came from Chris Grey-Wilson who gathered a few bulbs in Iran in 1964.

O. lacteum An attractive South African species which can reach about 90cm in height with a dense raceme of very large white flowers about 3–6cm in diameter. The leaves are short, up to 10cm long, and broadly lanceolate about 2–3cm wide although they do become more gross in cultivation. It grows wild in the south-west Cape. In Britain it should be treated as a cool greenhouse plant.

O. narbonense A very widespread species and very variable in stature. Usually about 30–50cm in height with the narrowly linear, channelled basal leaves rather greyish. The long raceme carries many flattish starry white or creamy flowers which have only a slight greenish stripe on the outside of the segments. The flowers are about 1–2cm in diameter. It occurs wild in Europe, especially around the Mediterranean, northern Africa and western Asia and is particularly common in Turkey and Iran, often in cultivated fields. Although not a showy plant, *O. narbonense* is a useful species flowering after the main display of spring bulbs. It requires a sunny position and well-drained soil. *O. pyramidale* is very similar.

O. nutans A rather distinctive species growing up to 30cm in height with long linear basal leaves. The raceme of flowers is almost a spike because of the very short pedicels. Each flower is about 2–2·5cm long, silvery-white with a very broad green stripe on the outside of the segments which are acute with an outward-curving tip. It occurs in Britain and Europe to western Turkey, although is probably native only in the Balkans. *O. boucheanum* from eastern Europe is almost identical in appearance and differs only in some obscure non-horticultural details concerning the stamens. *O. nutans* is a useful plant for naturalizing beneath shrubs as it is naturally a woodland plant.

O. pyrenaicum Grows up to 100cm in height with a very dense raceme 15–30cm long. The individual flowers are 1–1·5cm in diameter, very starry in appearance because of the narrow perianth segments, and are pale greeny-yellow with a darker green median stripe on each segment. The pedicels are 1–2cm long, more or less horizontal when the flowers are fully open, but becoming erect in the fruiting state. The tuft of narrowly linear basal leaves dies away at, or soon after, flowering time. Flowering June–July in the wild and in Britain. Occurs wild in southern England, central and southern Europe but not in the Balkans, although a similar plant occurs on Crete. The Spiked Star of Bethlehem, or the Bath Asparagus as it is often called, grows in grassy places at altitudes below 1300m. It is an easy plant in cultivation and requires only a partially sunny place, but it is not very showy and is less attractive than the somewhat similar but whitish-flowered *O. narbonense*.

O. reverchonii A robust species reaching 100cm in height with rather long, coarse leaves about 1·5cm wide. The large, 2cm wide, rather bell-shaped flowers are carried in a long raceme on fairly short pedicels and are creamy-white with only a slight hint of a green stripe along each segment. It occurs in rocky places or on ledges and crevices in south-west Spain at 800–1200m and flowers in May or June. This is one of the most striking of the European species of *Ornithogalum* and is easy to grow. I have not grown it outside for very long, having been rather cautious until I had sufficient bulbs to risk. However, for two winters it has remained undamaged through fairly hard frosts and I have hopes that it will be a useful garden plant.

O. saundersiae A robust grower reaching 75–100cm in height with several fairly erect, broad (up to 7cm), greyish-green basal leaves and a dense inflorescence which is rather compact with the lowest flowers on the longest pedicels. This has the effect of making all the flowers appear to be on the same level, although they are of course not produced in an umbel but a true raceme. Each creamy flower is flattish and 2·5–3cm in diameter with broad, rounded, perianth segments, brownish stamens and a blackish-green ovary, thus bearing some resemblance to *O. arabicum. O. saundersiae* is South African, from the Transvaal and Swaziland where it grows in humus-filled rock pockets below 1000m altitude. It is an attractive species for planting in a sunny border in spring, having been overwintered as dormant bulbs in a frost-free shed. In Britain it flowers in August and September.

O. subcucullatum This grows to about 50cm in height with a dense spike-like raceme of 1·5cm diameter short-pedicelled pure white flowers which lack the green external stripe so familiar in most of the European *Ornithogalum* species. Wild in the Gredos mountains of Spain where it grows at about 1700m in scrub and flowers in May or June. It needs a sheltered spot or bulb frame in most parts of Britain as it is probably slightly tender and requires a summer baking. The plant I know under this name was collected by Eliot Hodgkin, but it appears to be a poorly-known, little-collected species. *O. concinnum* is rather similar but more dwarf, reaching 30cm at most. It occurs in Portugal and Spain and requires bulb-frame cultivation.

O. thyrsoides The well-known Chincherinchee which makes a fine cut flower, being very long-lasting. It has many forms in the wild. The large white or cream flowers are cup-shaped, about 2·5cm in diameter, produced in long racemes up to about 70cm in height or in shorter, dense corymb-like inflorescences in some forms. The leaves are fairly variable but usually linear or lanceolate, 1–3cm wide and up to 40cm long. It is a native of the south-west Cape at low altitudes in seasonally moist grassy places, and is thus not hardy in Britain. However, it can be treated as summer-flowering here and the bulbs can be lifted for the winter and stored in a frost-free place until late spring. They require a sunny well-drained position, preferably in a rather sandy soil, and will flower in summer in Britain.

Pancratium Amaryllidaceae

A small but very exotic-looking genus which is, surprisingly, mainly Mediterranean in distribution, although some species spread through tropical Africa and India. They resemble the American species of *Hymenocallis* in having large, white scented flowers with a prominent cup formed from the expanded and joined filaments of the six stamens, while the perianth segments are rather narrow and usually standing out or a little recurved. The perianth tube is well developed, especially in the more tropical species. Although the Mediterranean species are of course by far the most useful in temperate gardens, and are actually more attractive than their tropical relatives, I am particularly fond of *P. tenuifolium* for nostalgic reasons. During an expedition to the Lake Rudolph area of northern Kenya I was camped near an apparently bare sandy area of several acres. After a shower one day the ground began to heave and in about 48 hours there were *Pancratium* and *Crinum* flowers everywhere! This species had only one or two flowers in each umbel. They were erect with a long tube and only night-flowering. Probably they are pollinated by moths, attracted by the fragrant white blooms. Of the Mediterranean species, *P. illyricum* is the hardiest, but even this is best grown in a frame or cool greenhouse unless the garden is in a very mild situation.

P. illyricum 30–45cm in height when in flower. Leaves widely strap-shaped, slightly glaucous. Flowers white, fragrant, ten to 15 in each umbel, rather starry and about 8cm in diameter with a short staminal cup. It occurs at low altitudes in the central Mediterranean and especially in Corsica where it grows in rocky places. May–June. I grew a bulb of this for several years in Surrey, planted hard up against a south-facing wall and it flowered every year until it finally succumbed in a severe winter. This came from Corsica and was brought by Sally (Maclagan) Walker. I now have another from Herbert and Molly Crook and will make sure that this one is well protected.

P. maritimum A very common species near the sea in the Mediterranean region. It is usually about 30cm in height and has narrower greyish-green leaves than *P. illyricum*. Flowers white, fragrant, up to six in each umbel, rather less substantial than those of *P. illyricum*, with flimsy white narrower segments and a longer cup. Nevertheless it is a beautiful and easy bulb for a cool greenhouse border or large pot. Sandy places, often on dunes by the sea, much more widespread around the Mediterranean than the preceding species. Flowers later, from July to September. *P. canariensis* is sometimes cultivated but is less hardy even than *P. maritimum* and must be given a little heat in winter. It has a short perianth tube and a shorter cup than either *P. maritimum* or *P. illyricum*.

P. parviflorum is sometimes referred to the genus *Vagaria* but is not very different in flower structure from typical *Pancratium*. The flowers are, as its name suggests, very much smaller than those of the other species and are tinged with green. It is a dwarf species, only reaching 20cm or so when in flower. The leaves are rather short and narrow, rather like those of *Sternbergia* but slightly greyish. It occurs at low altitudes at the eastern end of the Mediterranean, especially in Israel and neighbouring countries, and is too tender for cultivation outdoors in Britain.

Paramongaia Amaryllidaceae

A monotypic South American genus very closely resembling *Hymenocallis* and *Pancratium*. The comments made under the former genus apply here and there is no need to repeat them, except to say that *Paramongaia* differs mainly in having flat instead of swollen seeds. It needs a warm greenhouse and is a magnificent plant for pot cultivation, although very rare at present.

P. weberbaueri has bulbs like a large daffodil, producing 4cm wide, narrowly lanceolate, grey-green basal leaves. Flower-stem about 40–50cm in height with a few-flowered umbel of deep yellow, very fragrant flowers each with a spread of about 15–17cm. The six segments are 2–2·5cm wide and are about equal in length to the cup which is 10–12cm long and the segments join into an 8–10cm long tube. The only break in the intense flower colour is in the form of six green stripes along the cup where the filaments join on. In cultivation at Kew it flowered in September. Peru, on steep rocky hillsides at about 2700m.

Polianthes Agavaceae

It is curious that the beautiful and well-known Tuberose has been cultivated for at least 400 years and yet it is not known as a wild plant. There are eight other species, all from Mexico, and it seems likely that the origins of it are to be found there. It is possible that it is a selected clone of a wild species, and *P. gracilis* has been suggested in this connection. The genus *Bravoa*, which is split off from *Polianthes* by some botanists because of the red or orange flowers, contains three species and I have maintained them in this book as *Bravoa*. However they will be met with in some publications as *Polianthes* species. All the *Polianthes* have white or greenish-yellow flowers. Another genus which is very close is *P. rochnyanthes*, differing only slightly in having the filaments inserted below the bend in the perianth tube (above the bend in *Polianthes*). The long-tubular flowers of *Polianthes* are produced in a loose spike, in pairs in the axils of bracts, whereas the two genera *Manfreda* and *Pseudobravoa* both have solitary flowers in the axils. All of these genera incidentally differ from *Agave* in being herbaceous with a bulb-like rootstock, but are otherwise quite closely related. None of the *Polianthes* species is hardy in Britain but they can be grown in a cool greenhouse or planted out in May and lifted again for the winter.

P. durangensis Up to 50cm in height with several glabrous linear leaves up to 25cm long and 0·5cm wide, and about three short stem leaves. The nearly white flowers are sessile and are produced in a loose spike of about 4–6 pairs, each pair subtended by a bract. The perianth is 4–5cm long, strongly curved near the middle, and the spreading rounded lobes are about 8mm long. The stigma is included within the tube. Flowering August in Mexico, where it occurs on the Sierra Madre in the State of Durango. I am grateful to Fred Boutin of Los Angeles for my bulbs of this species.

P. gracilis For general description see *P. tuberosa*. This is very similar to *P. tuberosa* but has narrower leaves and is a more slender plant. J. N. Rose who revised *Polianthes* in 1903 stated that he was inclined to treat *P. gracilis* as the wild form from which the more robust *P. tuberosa* arose. I can find no trace of recent collections of *P. gracilis* although a plant, probably of this species, flowered as long ago as 1880 at Kew.

P. montana 120cm in height with several glaucous basal leaves 20–30cm long, 0·5–0·8cm wide, and about six small stem leaves. Inflorescence of 12 pairs of shortly stalked white flowers 1·5–2cm long, with the tube slightly curved from the base. The small rounded lobes are not spreading. I have not seen this species. It was first collected by Rose on the Sierra Madre of Mexico, flowering in August.

P. nelsonii is rather like *P. durangensis* in general characters but has leaves which are finely-toothed on the margin and narrowly ovate bracts (broadly ovate in the latter); the stigma is exserted from the tube, and the lobes are shorter. Mexico, Durango; flowering in August.

P. palustris has basal leaves 1·2–1·5cm wide with a distinct petiole and in these broad leaves it differs from all the other species. Otherwise it is similar to *P. durangensis* but has shorter lobes, 0·5–0·6mm long, and a less strongly curved tube. It is said to be strongly perfumed. Mexico, Sierra Madre, where it was originally gathered in swampy ground.

P. pringlei has leaves only 0·1–0·3cm wide. The flowers are similar to those of *P. durangensis*, but the lobes are linear and unequal, the lower one 1–1·5cm long. Mexico, on moist hills near Guadalajara, flowering in August. I do not know of this species being cultivated, although in the early part of this century it was sold in the markets near its wild locality and must be an attractive plant.

P. sessiliflora Very close to *P. durangensis* but with a few very narrow leaves about 0·2cm wide and flowers 3–4cm long, curved near the base. The lobes are about 0·4cm long. It was first collected in Mexico in 1878 at San Luis Potosi.

P. tuberosa This is by far the best-known species but is usually only obtainable nowadays in its double form which is to my mind less attractive than the single. It grows up to 100cm in height. Basal leaves several, up to 50cm long, 0·5–1·5cm broad. Flowers in a lax spike, fragrant and white, waxy in texture, with a tube 3cm long, curved near the base; lobes 1·5cm long. As mentioned above, this is not known in the wild but may be a selection of *P. gracilis*. It has been cultivated at least since the sixteenth century and was at one time much more widely grown in Britain than it is at present. There is a long account of its cultivation in the early nineteenth century in Britain by R. A. Salisbury in the Transactions of the Horticultural Society of London (1812). The single form was known to Clusius in 1594, and the double was mentioned as long ago as 1731. Obviously the tuberose was a very popular plant, for Salisbury commented that in ¼ acre plot it was possible to grow 15,125 roots, which at 3d each was £189.1s.6d. After deduction of overheads 'the profits of a bed of tuberoses would be considerable'! Briefly, the method of cultivation consisted of planting the tubers just beneath the surface in a very rich soil, at the foot of a south wall. The soil recommended was light, sandy, mixed with a third of well-rotted cow manure. Before planting in April the bed was dug out to a depth of 2½ feet, part-filled with fresh stable dung and then topped up with the manure-rich soil again. The bed was covered with matting until the leaves emerged and then watered freely until the autumn. After flowering, and before December, the bed was cleared of the old growths and thatched with straw for the winter. Alternatively, it seems that the tubers could be lifted and stored in sand for the winter, repeating the planting process in April. Salisbury also recommends cutting out all but two or three side-growths before planting. In the early nineteenth century, gardeners obviously found more time to lavish upon their plants!

Prochnyanthes Agavaceae

A small genus of Mexican plants closely related to *Polianthes* but differing in having the filaments inserted below the bend in the perianth tube (above it in *Polianthes*). Like this genus and *Bravoa*, *Prochnyanthes* needs to be cultivated in a cool greenhouse in Britain, or lifted for the winter and the bulbs stored in sand in a frost-free environment.

P. viridescens has a bulb about 5cm long, clothed with the fibres of old leaves. Stems up to 150cm high. Basal leaves many, up to 5cm broad, slightly glaucous; stem leaves becoming smaller towards the top of the stem. Inflorescence a raceme consisting of up to 30 pairs of greenish or brownish flowers each on a pedicel up to 4cm long, but sometimes very short. The curved tube is about 4cm long and is considerably expanded just above the middle so that the upper half is bell-like, with spreading lobes. Widespread in Mexico where it grows in grassy places and flowers in August and September. This is definitely a bulb enthusiast's plant, for it has no great claim to beauty! It is probable that this is the only species, for although two other names have been given to specimens, *P. bulliana* and *P. mexicana*, they sound exactly like *P. viridescens* from their descriptions.

Pseudobravoa Agavaceae

A Mexican genus of one species related to *Bravoa* and *Polianthes*, differing mainly in having a short dense spike of flowers which are produced singly in the axils of long tapering bracts. The only other genus in the group of genera related to *Polianthes* which has solitary flowers in the axils of the bracts is *Manfreda*. *Pseudobravoa*, however, has the stamens hidden within the tube, and a dense inflorescence, while *Manfreda* has the stamens protruding and has a more lax inflorescence. Unfortunately I have not yet tried to grow this species and can only comment from herbarium material.

P. densiflora has a very loose scaly bulb with a mass of rather thick fleshy roots from the base-plate. The short leaves are very narrowly linear and are produced in a basal tuft of up to ten, overtopped by the inflorescence which reaches 15–45cm. The spike is rather short and dense, giving an almost head-like appearance, especially as the flowers open from the base first and are more or less erect so that the tips of the open flowers and the buds are at the same level. The yellow flowers are 5–6cm long, tubular, rather curved with very short lobes. North-west Mexico, up to 2600m in meadows. Flowering late summer in the wild.

Pseudogaltonia Liliaceae

An African genus of one species, according to the Prodromus Flora of South-West Africa, *P. clavata*, (*P. subspicata*, *P. pechuelii*).

P. clavata has a large bulb up to 17cm in diameter with the scales separating into strong coarse fibres, especially at the apex. Leaves more or less lanceolate, up to ten in number, upright, usually absent or very short at flowering time, eventually up to 30cm long and 9cm wide. Inflorescence 40–60cm high with a dense raceme up to 25cm long. Flowers rather funnel-shaped on pedicels 2–3cm long, white with a greenish suffusion, up to 3·5cm long with a slightly curved tube over half the length of the flower. Namaqualand, South-West Africa and probably Angola, where it flowers from October to December. It differs from *Galtonia* in having stamens attached in the throat of the flower, not down in the tube as in *Galtonia*.

It has never been well known in Britain and is never likely to be, for it is not hardy and is rather less attractive than any of the Galtonias. Nevertheless, for those interested in cool greenhouse plants it is quite striking and should be planted out in a bed rather than pot-grown, for it is a robust plant. It was cultivated as long ago as 1881 at Kew and was figured for the *Botanical Magazine* in 1886.

Rigidella Iridaceae

A small central American genus with all species having very striking but short-lived scarlet flowers. It is related to *Tigridia* and apart from the flower colour (no *Tigridia* is the same bright red) and the fact that the flowers of *Rigidella* are pollinated by humming-birds and those of *Tigridia* are visited by flies or bees, it is difficult to state exactly what are the distinguishing features. The flowers consist of three large outer segments and three smaller inner ones, as in *Tigridia*, but in *Rigidella* the expanded blades of the outer segments reflex sharply. The filaments are joined into a long tube surrounding the long slender style. Robert Cruden has discussed more fully the differences between the two genera in a revision of the genus in *Brittonia* 23 no 2: 217 (1971) and I am grateful to Dr Cruden for some of the information gleaned from his paper. I have grown only one species successfully so far, *R. orthantha*, and this is not at all difficult although my own plants have been grown in a cool greenhouse border. At Kew it has grown and flowered for several years at the base of a warm wall, and it was successfully cultivated in the garden of the late Lord Talbot de Malahide near Dublin. Four species are known at present, although I have heard that there are some new ones awaiting description. They can be divided into those with pendulous flowers (*R. immaculata* and *R. flammea*) and those with erect flowers (*R. orthantha* and *R. inusitata*).

R. flammea A robust plant up to 100cm in height with two or three pleated lanceolate basal leaves which are short at flowering time but reach over 100cm by fruiting time; stem leaves much shorter. Inflorescence enclosed within spathes which produce up to 15 flowers in succession, each lasting a few hours in the afternoon (all the other species open in the morning). Flowers nodding, the lower part of the segments forming a cup about 2cm deep and the upper part sharply reflexed in a cyclamen-like fashion. The yellow inner segments are held within the cup while the stamens and style protrude a long way beyond it. The colour is deep red, spotted and lined black around the cup, and the whole flower is about 5cm long from the tips of the reflexed segments to the tips of the protruding anthers. Mexico, in open rocky places in forests up to 2300m. To date I have not been very successful with this species, but there is no apparent reason why it should be more difficult than *R. orthantha* which I find easy to grow.

R. immaculata Like *R. flammea* this also has pendulous flowers but these are unspotted, rather smaller, about 4cm between the extremities of the segments and have a more shallow cup, up to 1.5cm deep; the basal leaves are fully developed by flowering time, up to about 90cm in length. Mexico and Guatemala in grassy places in the damp forest regions between 2000 and 3300m.

R. inusitata Only described in 1971 by R. W. Cruden, this is one of the species with erect flowers, but also has reflexed segments. About 90cm in height with two basal leaves up to 65cm long and one shorter stem leaf. Flowers irregular in shape, the reflexed segments all held to one side, about 8cm long from the tips of the segments to the tips of the anthers and stigma. The cup is about 1cm deep and the inner segments are held within this. *R. inusitata* differs from all the other species in having irregular flowers with displaced stamens, a feature which makes for very certain pollination by visiting birds, according to Cruden. Mexico, in Guerrero State in damp rock areas from 2670–3600m.

R. orthantha also has erect flowers with reflexed outer segments but is immediately recognizable because of the upright, yellow, inner segments which protrude from the cup and are clearly visible. The cup is about 1–1·2cm deep and the whole flower about 6cm long between the extremities of anthers and segments. This is a robust plant about the same size as *R. flammea* but the basal leaves are well developed at flowering time, and the floral characters are quite different. Mexico and Guatemala, in mountains above 2650m in the cloud forest region. As mentioned above, this is a very satisfactory and showy plant for a warm situation. In the growing season it needs a lot of moisture, but in the winter dormant period is best kept a little on the dry side.

R. orthantha has been hybridized with *Tigridia pavonia* to produce an extremely vigorous sterile plant intermediate between the parents. The erect flowers have the outer segments scarlet and reflexing as in *R. orthantha* while the smaller inner yellow ones are larger than in *Rigidella*, showing the influence of *Tigridia*.

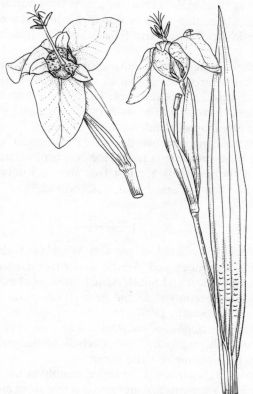

29 *Tigridia pavonia* × *Rigidella orthantha*

The cup is large like that of *Tigridia pavonia*, spotted and blotched scarlet and yellow. In its flower characters it is no real improvement horticulturally on either parent but it increases by bulb division so rapidly and flowers so freely from June until August that it is a worthwhile plant to grow. The flowers open during the early morning. My own plants have always been in a deep pot or planted out in the cool greenhouse but it should be tried out of doors.

Sandersonia Liliaceae

A monotypic genus from southern Africa, obviously related to *Gloriosa* but easily distinguished. The solitary species is easily cultivated in a frost-free greenhouse and does especially well if planted out in the borders but can be equally well grown in deep pots. The finger-like tubers should be kept dryish in winter and started into growth in early spring. The soft young shoots appear in April and this is the time when protection is necessary, otherwise the species would be fairly hardy out of doors. If grown in pots they can be placed outside after the danger of frost is over and make attractive plants for a patio. The weak stems require some support from thin canes or pea-sticks. In mild areas the tubers can be planted outside in April in a warm border and lifted again when dormant before winter.

S. aurantiaca reaches about 75cm in cultivation with thin stems carrying scattered, lanceolate, bright green leaves which clasp the stem and which usually have tendrils at their tips. Each of the upper leaves has a flower in its axil, borne on a slender pedicel 2–3cm long. The six perianth segments are fused together to form an inflated urn-shaped, pendulous, bright orange flower, 2–2·5cm long, which has the mouth facing downwards and six prominent spurs on the base pointing upwards; these spurs are in reality the deeply pitted nectaries inside the flower. The tips of the segments are just free and curl outwards. Flowering June–July in Britain. Eastern Cape, Natal, Lesotho and Swaziland, 600–2000m.

Scilla Liliaceae

A large genus, widely distributed in the Old World and although generally thought of as being European and Asiatic by British gardeners, there are a number of species in tropical and South Africa. Most of these southern hemisphere species have been removed to the genus *Ledebouria* by Jessop in the *Journal of South African Botany* (1970) but a few remain, including one of the most striking of the taller *Scillas*, *S. natalensis*. There are very few which can be said to be tall, so with the removal of the Bluebells to the genus *Hyacinthoides* there remains very little for me to write about!

The characteristics of *Scilla* are to be found mainly in the flowers, the chief being that the perianth segments are more or less free from each other, and the stamen filaments, which are also free, are not expanded as in *Puschkinia* and

30 *Sandersonia aurantiaca*

Chionodoxa. Urginea is a very closely related genus and rather difficult to separate on morphological grounds. One can generalize however and say that
practically all of the true *Scillas* have blue or purple flowers, while *Urginea*
never has flowers in this colour range. Similarly, *Ornithogalum* usually has
white flowers with a few yellow ones in South Africa.

S. hispanica See *Hyacinthoides hispanica*.

S. hughii See *S. peruviana*.

S. hyacinthoides This has a very large bulb up to 8cm in diameter and grows up
to 90cm in height when in flower. The leaves are channelled, up to 2·5cm wide
and as much as 40cm in length at flowering time and are produced in an erect
basal rosette of up to eight in number. The raceme produces numerous lilac or
bluebell-blue rather 'starry' flowers, each about 1cm in diameter with the

perianth segments spread out flat and non-overlapping. They are each carried on a slender pedicel up to 3·5cm in length, the pedicels and flower stem often coloured blue like the flowers. It grows in rocky places and in fields around the Mediterranean from Portugal to Israel, never at very high altitudes, although just reaching 1000m in the east of its range in Iraq and south-east Turkey. Flowering April–May. I have not been very successful in flowering this species, although it grows well enough amongst the *Iris unguicularis* against a south wall. It undoubtedly requires a very hot position.

S. lilio-hyacinthus An interesting species 15–25cm in height, very distinct from other *Scillas* in having a lily-like bulb with rather loose scales. The leaves are oblanceolate, up to 2·5cm broad, produced in an erect basal rosette. The dense raceme carries many blue flowers about 1·5cm in diameter. It grows wild in western Europe in woods at up to 2000m and in cultivation seems to grow well in slight shade, especially on chalky soils. It flowers in May or June in Britain.

S. natalensis From a bulb up to 10cm in diameter a rosette of rather stiff, lanceolate, strongly-veined leaves are produced, and a long inflorescence up to 80cm in height. The raceme of flowers is 20–30cm in length and carries masses of starry blue (sometimes pink or white) flowers 1·5–2cm in diameter. The ovary and style in the form I know are white, so that the flower appears to have a white eye. The pedicels are held horizontally and are coloured the same blue as the

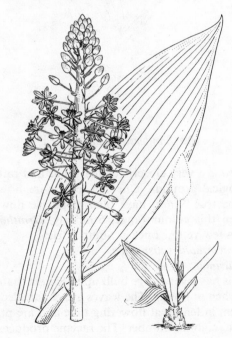

31 *Scilla natalensis*

flowers. At flowering time the leaves are only 15–20cm in length but eventually they may expand to up to 60cm long and 7cm broad. It is native of the eastern parts of southern Africa in the Transvaal, Natal, the Orange Free State and Lesotho, where it inhabits grassy and rocky places in damp acid soils from about 800–2000m. In England it flowers in July and is best grown in a cool greenhouse where the dormant bulbs will be frost-free in winter. It is hardy in very mild areas and should be grown in a hot sunny position.

S. non-scripta See *Hyacinthoides non-scripta*.

S. peruviana Although not very tall, this has fairly massive proportions. The large bulbs are best planted with their tops at soil level. The linear-lanceolate leaves are produced in a dense sub-erect basal rosette. The 1·5–2cm diameter flowers are very numerous, carried in a broadly conical raceme 15–25cm in height and are a rather steely dark blue; an albino form is known. The lower pedicels are about 4cm long, elongating to 9cm in the fruiting stage. It is wild in Portugal, Spain and Italy in moist grassy places at low altitudes. In Britain it flowers in May or June and requires a hot sunny position to flower well. *S. hughii* is rather similar but even larger in all its parts.

Stenomesson Amaryllidaceae

Rather exotic-looking South American bulbs with umbels of pendulous, tubular, or occasionally more bell-shaped flowers, in bright colours. They are cool greenhouse plants, but as some of them come from the high Andes it might be worth trying them in very mild areas against a warm wall. Unfortunately they flower in winter in Britain so that it is unlikely that they will be very successful. The leaves are strap-like and are produced basally in one plane from a large bulb, which in most species has several offsets. The inflorescence often appears just before the leaves. One of the species I have tried seems to be fairly hardy in a very slightly heated greenhouse so it might be worth trying it outside. This is the very variable *S. variegatum* which probably includes *S. incarnatum* and *S. luteoviride*. The forms I have grown have all been similar to each other except for their flower colour. The four to eight bluish-green leaves are strap-shaped, 60–70cm long when mature but usually quite short at flowering time, and are spreading to recurved. In flower the height of the plant is about 40–60cm with the stem central among the leaves and carrying an umbel of six to eight flowers. The flower has a long down-curved tube causing the flower to be rather drooping, and is about 4–7cm long and 1cm wide at the mouth. The perianth segments are ovate, about 1·5–2·5cm long, spreading out from the apex of the tube. Joined to the base of the segments are the stamens which have flattened filaments provided with a tooth on either side of the anthers. The colour varies enormously and this probably accounts for quite a lot of 'species' within the genus. On the perianth segments there is always a green blotch, but the tube can be greenish-yellow, soft yellow, tawny yellow with reddish bands, pink with deeper red bands, crimson, rose or wholly scarlet. *S. variegatum* occurs wild in the South American Andes of Ecuador, Peru and Bolivia at altitudes of 3000–4200m in stony places. In Britain it usually flowers in March in my experience, and sometimes again in July. Other species which I have tried seem to be less tolerant of cool temperatures although I must admit to not having experimented very much with their cultivation.

Tigridia Iridaceae

The majority of *Tigridia* species occur in central America, in Mexico and Guatemala, and a well-illustrated monograph by Dr Elwood Molseed was published in 1970 (University of California Publications, in *Botany*, vol. 54). Only one species, *T. pavonia*, is at all well known in cultivation although several more have been introduced in recent years and are settling down now that their requirements are better understood. None of the species rivals *T. pavonia* in gaudiness but some are much more attractive in a subtle way and I can only repeat my statement in *Dwarf Bulbs* that they are fascinating additions to any bulb collection. The flowers are very short-lived, *Iris*-like in general shape, with three large outer segments, together with the three smaller inner ones forming a cup in which there are nectar-bearing glands. In a few species the segments are nearly equal, and the flowers may be upright or pendulous. The leaves are usually rather narrow and distinctly pleated.

Tigridias are not hardy in cold areas but will survive most winters in the extreme south and south-west of England. In very favourable areas they will seed freely and become more or less naturalized, as they have in a garden I know in Somerset. The Central American species are summer-growing, flowering in mid to late summer and becoming dormant in winter when they should be kept dry. I have succeeded best with them planted out in a border in a frost-free greenhouse. Among the taller species I have grown are:

T. bicolor This reaches 25–40cm in height and has one or two long narrow leaves, longer than the inflorescence. Flowers erect, 2–2·5cm in diameter, many being produced in succession from each set of bracts. The cup-shaped centre of the flower is brownish-purple and the larger flattened portion of the outer segments (the 'falls') is yellow. Wild in Oaxaca, Mexico between 2000–2500m. As with many of my *Tigridias*, I have Sally Walker to thank for sending me this. It is an attractive species, with its strikingly bicoloured flowers and has set seeds without hand-pollination in my greenhouse. Unlike many species, it grows in rather dry places and certainly did best when I had it growing in a sandy bed in my frost-free greenhouse, with little shading in summer.

T. chiapensis Although this was included in *Dwarf Bulbs*, I include it here also as it can reach 40cm, although is usually less. It has upright flowers about 4–5cm in diameter, white with a yellow, purple-spotted centre, the three outer segments being much larger than the inner. It occurs wild in a rather restricted area in Chiapas, Mexico from 1300–3000m in wet meadows. It would be worth trying this outside in warmer districts where the frosts are not too severe, but so far I have not dared to risk it.

T. ehrenbergii This is one of the least exciting species I have grown, with smallish pendulous flowers on a plant up to 80cm in height. There are many flowers in succession, each about 2·5–3·5cm in diameter, with the three outer segments much larger than the inner, giving a snowdrop-shaped appearance. They are yellowish, spotted faintly with purple. Wild in central Mexico from 1300–2300m in dry scrub and light woodland.

T. galanthoides Perhaps the name of this is more enticing than the plant! It is not unlike *T. ehrenbergii* in general stature and appearance but the flowers are smaller, only 1–2cm in diameter, and even more snowdrop-like in shape. It is very aptly named, for the pendulous flowers have three long, rather rounded, segments and three short inner ones, but there the similarity ends, for the colour is pale pink or whitish with darker veining so pronounced that it gives the flower a more pinkish appearance. The rather lanky flower-stem is branched and each branch has a terminal set of bracts which enclose many flowers so that often there are several flowers out each day. Occurs wild mainly in the Oaxaca State of Mexico at around 2000–2500m in rocky, grassy or wooded places. I have not grown this for long but it seems to be easy in my cool greenhouse, planted out among other tender summer-rainfall bulbs. It flowers freely and usually sets seed, although the very hot dry summer of 1976 discouraged most of the *Tigridia* species from doing so and they went prematurely dormant.

T. meleagris A fascinating species with flower-stems 25–60cm in height and nodding, rather *Fritillaria*-like flowers about 2–3cm in diameter with all six segments roughly equal in size. The colour is pinkish with darker spots and blotches and the recurved pointed tips of the three inner segments are yellow. Wild in central Mexico and the mountains of Guatemala, between 1300–2300m in grassy and lightly wooded places. In cultivation in Britain it has shown a preference for shade, the foliage becoming scorched in my unshaded greenhouse.

T. multiflora One of the smaller upright-flowered species, up to 50cm in height with brownish-orange to purple flowers 3–4cm in diameter. These have the outer segments about twice the size of the inner and they together form a deep-ish cup with their basal portions, while the upper half of each bends sharply outwards and stands out more or less horizontally or slightly reflexed. Mountains of north and central Mexico at 1800–3000m in dryish wooded areas.

T. pavonia The most well-known species, forming the illustration for the dust cover and frontispiece of *Dwarf Bulbs*. One must admit, however, that it is not very dwarf and could equally adorn the front of this book! Reaches 50cm in height with a fan of rather broad, pleated basal leaves and a few stem leaves. Flowers very large and showy, much the largest and gaudiest in the genus, 10–15cm in diameter. Very variable in colour in reds, orange, yellow or white, all with or without red blotches in the centre. The six segments form a cup but the outer are very much larger than the inner and have horizontal or reflexed blades which give it the appearance of a very exotic *Iris*. Various names exist for the colour variants but it is better to keep raising mixed batches from seed as the species is very prone to virus troubles if the old bulbs are retained. It can be flowered in one season from seed and is hardy in southern England, although it may succumb in severe winters, certainly in the south-east. The most vigorous form I have was a wild collected one sent by Sally Walker in a really brilliant orange scarlet. The plain yellow ones are particularly attractive, while the most extraordinary is one which Mrs Walker bought in a drug store in Arizona. Thinking it would be the 'ordinary' form I planted it out in the greenhouse and forgot about it, only to be amazed one day to see an unspotted flower of a most curious shade of red with a rim of yellow around the cup and yellow tips to the inner three segments. Needless to say we have, somewhat unbotanically, dubbed it 'Drugstorensis'! *T. pavonia* occurs wild in Mexico and Guatemala but is now naturalized in many parts of South America and in other tropical and sub-tropical areas. It is usually known as the Tiger Flower but also as Jockey-Cap in New Zealand.

T. vanhouttei A rather smallish-flowered species, but very easy to grow and setting seed freely. It reaches 60cm in height with a few-branched inflorescence but has a long succession of flowers from each set of bracts. Flowers more or less erect 2–3cm in diameter, deeply cupped, with the three outer segments larger than the inner and having a horizontal blade, strongly veined dark purple on a pale yellowish ground. It is wild in Central Mexico, especially the valley of Mexico, at 2000–2500m in rather dry rocky places. It is unfortunate that *T. vanhouttei* is a rather dull species, for with me it has proved to be more persistent than most of the others.

T. violacea Usually rather a compact species while in flower, but reaching 45cm. Flowers 3–5cm in diameter, upright, with the large blade of the outer segments sharply reflexed from the edge of the cup, bright purple, shading to whitish or yellow and spotted with purple inside the cup. Central Mexico in grassland at around 2000m and above. This flowered for the first time in my cool greenhouse in 1976 and proved to be most attractive. It is rather early flowering, in June–July, compared with most of the others I have grown.

In addition to these I have several other species given to me by Sally Walker, Caryn Ecker and Robert Cruden, but as they have not yet settled down in cultivation it seems unwise to extol their virtues!

Trillium Liliaceae

Beautiful woodland plants from North America and eastern Asia. They are very hardy and easily grown in Britain, being very suited to cool shady sites in a not too dry climate. They are ideal for the rock garden or peat garden and the larger species look very attractive in a woodland setting. As the name suggests, the parts of the plant are in threes, with three stem leaves in a whorl, three outer greenish perianth segments and three inner segments which are large and showy. The root consists of a thick rhizome which can be divided when clumps have formed. Seed is produced freely and should be sown immediately it is gathered. I have grown several species, but only three which come near the category of 'larger bulbs'.

T. cernuum Rather a small-flowered species about 25–45cm in height with broad leaves. The flowers are drooping on weak pedicels and are about 2–3cm in diameter, white or pinkish. It occurs wild in the eastern states of America and Canada.

T. grandiflorum The Wake Robin. This is probably the finest of all the *Trilliums*, up to about 40cm in height with plain green, broadly ovate leaves. The flowers are pure white or rose-flushed, about 6–12cm in diameter and carried on a 5cm pedicel. It grows wild in eastern and central North America. There is a beautiful tightly double form in cultivation which is uncommon and expensive at present. *T. ovatum* from the western United States is very similar but with smaller flowers in which the perianth segments spread from the base, whereas in *T. grandiflorum* they are erect at the base and spread out in the upper three-quarters of the segments.

T. sessile This grows up to 25cm in height with large oval leaves, beautifully mottled. The deep reddish-purple flowers have erect segments and are 3–4cm long and completely lacking a pedicel, hence the name. Var. *luteum* has yellowish-green flowers. *T. sessile* is widespread in North America.

Triteleia Liliaceae

This is an American genus, closely allied to *Brodiaea* and the details of the botanical differences will be found under that genus, together with the cultural recommendations. The species mostly flower in May to July in Britain and lose their long linear leaves at about the same time or earlier so that the flower-stems look rather bare. They are mostly 25–40cm in height when in flower.

T. bridgesii This has large umbels about 10cm in diameter containing up to 30 flowers which are carried on long pedicels, 4–6cm in length. The narrowly funnel-shaped flowers are deep blue-purple, about 3·5cm long, 2cm of which is the perianth tube. The lobes spread to give the flower a diameter at the mouth of about 2–2·5cm. It grows wild in California and Oregon.

T. grandiflora The flowers of this species are on rather short pedicels up to 3cm in length, giving the umbel a fairly compact appearance. Each flower is about 2cm long, the tube being 1cm long, and is widely funnel-shaped and mid-blue. The diameter at the mouth is about 2cm. It is widespread in the western states of America on grassy slopes and rock outcrops.

T. hyacinthina (*Brodiaea lactea*) This has dense umbels up to 7cm in diameter with the flowers on pedicels up to 3cm long. The colour is whitish and the flowers are

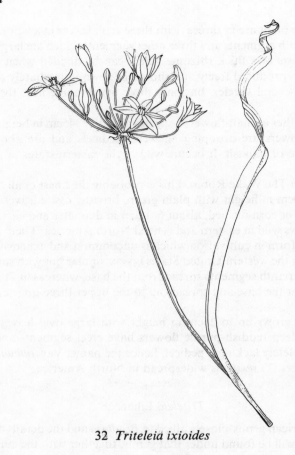

32 *Triteleia ixioides*

about 7cm in length and 2cm across at the mouth, with a very short tube. It grows wild in the western United States, from British Columbia south to California, in damp grassy places. It is an easy species in cultivation and is quite showy.

T. ixioides A yellow species with up to 20 flowers on 4–5cm pedicels, giving the umbel a spread of up to 10cm. The individual flowers are starry and 1·5–2cm in diameter with a very short perianth tube. The perianth segments usually have a purplish stripe running down the middle. It grows wild in grassy places in California and Oregon.

T. laxa A large-flowered species and one of the most striking. The deep blue flowers are up to 3cm in diameter and 2·5–4cm long including the perianth tube which is 2–2·5cm long. The umbel is 6–16cm in diameter and many-flowered but appears to be rather loose because the pedicels are up to 8cm in length. It is wild in California and Oregon in grassy places.

T. × *tubergenii* This is considered to be a hybrid between *T. laxa* and *T. pedunculata* but is very similar to some forms of *T. laxa*. It is a vigorous plant and very easy to grow in a warm sunny situation. One of the many fine plants raised by van Tubergen Ltd. The flowers are rich blue-lilac and the stems and peduncles are very stout.

Tulipa Liliaceae

The beautiful species of tulip have a grace and charm which is often lacking in the large-flowered garden hybrids, although for display purposes in large bedding arrangements these are, of course, superior. The genus is a difficult one taxonomically and a revision is badly needed. The main problem is the extreme variability within one species and it is possible to find many colours, shapes and sizes in one population. The attractive monograph of the genus, *The Genus Tulipa* by A. D. Hall (RHS, 1940) is still the main reference work but is somewhat outdated in the light of the many recent introductions.

Only a small percentage of the known species are in cultivation and it is mainly through the efforts of the firm of van Tubergen that so many are available. Mr Michael Hoog, lately of that firm, has been responsible for bringing in many of the Russian species during recent years. To attempt to cover the genus comprehensively here would be quite impossible, even confining myself to the taller species, so I have dealt with the more well-known ones only.

Cultivation of most species consists of growing the bulbs on a well-drained sunny site, planting them in late autumn. Unless the climate is a normally particularly warm one in summer it is best to lift the bulbs during their dormant period and to store them in a temperature of at least 65°F. This gives them a thorough ripening and flowering is more reliable. Bulb-frame cultivation is very suitable, but of course the taller species need a lot of headroom and space which is better reserved for more compact species of bulb. Propagation is by seed or by vegetative bulb division. The former method is laborious since it takes anything from four to seven years for seedlings to reach flowering size. Most of the taller tulips flower in April and May and have solitary upward-facing flowers.

T. acuminata A curious-looking plant which is unknown in the wild and is probably an old, well-established hybrid. It grows to about 40cm in height and the 7–8cm long flower has long narrow perianth segments tapering to a twisted point. The colour is a peculiar mixture of pale tomato-red, yellow, and a touch of green.

T. clusiana The Lady Tulip. A beautiful tulip which has been in cultivation for at least 370 years, for Clusius notes flowering it in 1607. It is a polyploid plant derived, according to Hall, from *T. aitchisonii*, a native of the mountains of Chitral and Kashmir. *T. chitralensis* is another polyploid of similar appearance. *T. clusiana* has two 1cm wide grey-green basal leaves and two narrower leaves on the 30cm stem. The flower is about 5cm long with pointed segments, opening to a flat starry shape, and is white with a central eye of dark purple inside, crimson-stained on the outside. It is naturalized on the Mediterranean coast of France but is unknown as a wild plant. The wild species, *T. aitchisonii*, is rather smaller in its stature and flowers but is otherwise rather similar, occurring in both the white form and one which has a yellow ground colour with red on the exterior but has no purple central eye. *T. stellata* is another related species from Afghanistan and north-west India which is either white or yellow, stained with red on the exterior. The central blotch in this plant is yellow. The yellow form of *T. stellata* is known as var. *chrysantha*, sometimes the whole group being referred to as varieties of *T. clusiana*, i.e. *T. clusiana* var. *stellata* and *T. clusiana* var. *chrysantha*. Although inhabitants of hot dry mountain slopes, they grow well in Britain given a warm well-drained spot such as at the foot of a south wall.

T. eichleri A gaudy species up to 30cm in height with broad grey leaves. The flowers are up to 12cm in diameter with broad segments, the colour being an intense scarlet with a yellow-margined black basal blotch in the centre. It occurs in Iran and Russian Tadjikistan on hot dry slopes. In a warm border it will last for several years in Britain without lifting. *T. ingens* is very similar but has a hairy stem (glabrous in *T. eichleri*) and no yellow margin to the basal blotch. *T. tubergeniana* also has a pubescent stem but here the black blotch is margined with yellow, as in *T. eichleri*, and the inner perianth segments are more rounded than in either of the other two species. Both *T. ingens* and *T. tubergeniana* occur wild in Russian Central Asia.

T. fosterana A well-known species, available in many different cultivars now. It grows 20–45cm in height with broad grey leaves. In some variants the flowers reach 20cm in diameter but most are much smaller than this. The wild form has broad perianth segments of a brilliant scarlet-red with a blackish basal blotch margined with yellow. It grows wild in Uzbekistan and Tadjikistan. Named cultivars can be found in bulb catalogues, differing in flower colour, size and stature, but in addition to the variants of *T. fosterana* itself there are hybrids between this and other species, notably *T. greigii* which imparts some of its attractive foliage features to them. Although an easy species to grow in Britain, *T. fosterana* is best lifted each year and given a warm dry period of dormancy.

T. gesnerana A common tulip in Asia Minor, naturalized in parts of the Mediterranean and of uncertain status. It is generally considered to be one of an ancient race of tulips, probably of garden origin, which are now firmly established in apparently wild situations. I remember seeing fields in central Turkey literally covered with red tulips of all shapes and sizes, looking like some nurseryman's neglected stock-bed. It grows to about 30–45cm in height with several broad, slightly greyish-green leaves, the upper ones narrow and scattered up the stem. The flowers of the Turkish plants answering to this name are scarlet-red with a yellow-margined basal blotch inside, rather cup-shaped with pointed segments. It is very easy to grow and need not be lifted for the summer.

T. greigii This is a very popular tulip for it flowers early and has a wide range of colourful cultivars which are reasonably priced. The wild plant grows to about 20–30cm in height, but some of the cultivars exceed this, and has broad leaves beautifully mottled and streaked with dark purple. The flowers are rather open cup-shaped when fully out, up to 15cm in diameter, brilliant scarlet to yellow with an orange stain on the exterior and a blackish, yellow-margined blotch in the centre. In its native Tadjikistan it grows on hot rocky slopes. Like *T. fosterana* it is best lifted for storing in a warm dry place in summer. Many cultivars are offered now and it is best to refer to up-to-date catalogues for the latest selection.

T. hageri Although less gaudy than the flamboyant Middle Asian species, *T. hageri* is nevertheless rather attractive. The height is usually about 25–40cm with narrow green leaves in a basal cluster and a few scattered up the stem. The 6–9cm diameter flowers are dull red with a greenish-black, yellow-margined centre and a green band running the length of the segments externally. *T. orphanidea* is very similar, perhaps a little larger with more slender flowers of a slightly more bronze colour with green at the centre. Both occur in Greece in the mountains, often in fields or on rocky grassy hillsides. *T. whittallii* from western Turkey is also related to these and differs only in having a slightly more robust habit, orange-red flowers with a green and biscuit-coloured exterior and a deep olive green central blotch. It is probable that it cannot be separated specifically from *T. hageri*.

T. hoogiana Commemorating one of the famous names of the tulip world, this is a beautiful, striking species growing up to 45cm in height with a huge flower 15–20cm in diameter when fully open. It is brilliant orange-red with a black, yellow-margined, basal blotch. The basal leaves are broad and grey-green, the upper stem-leaves much narrower. It is a late-flowering tulip, often into May. Although a native of Turkmenistan, where it has cold winters – and is therefore hardy enough in Britain – it does also experience hot dry summers and in our climate needs to be lifted for a warm dry rest period.

T. kolpakowskiana This is usually less than 30cm in height with the greyish basal leaves narrow and wavy-margined. The flowers have narrow, pointed segments and are 6–8cm in diameter when fully open. Although the form in cultivation has yellow flowers stained with carmine on the exterior, it is apparently very variable in the wild from yellow to red. It occurs in Russia, east of the Caspian Sea.

T. marjolettii This is probably not a true wild species, but one of the old garden hybrids which has established itself in parts of southern France. It is an attractive plant of easy culture and has the graceful appearance of a *Tulipa* species even if it is of dubious background. The height is usually about 35–45cm, with grey leaves and a soft primrose-yellow flower with slight reddish staining on the exterior.

T. praecox A robust species of unknown wild origin which is now naturalized in Italy and southern France. It grows 30–60cm in height, with broad grey leaves and a large scarlet-red flower with a dark olive green basal blotch, outlined with yellow. The perianth segments are unequal in size, the outer being noticeably larger than the inner. It has a stoloniferous habit, so in the right situations has the possibility of spreading freely. It requires a hot sunny position on well-drained soil, preferably alkaline.

T. praestans This is unusual among the red-flowered tulips in having several flowers per stem. The height is up to 30cm, with broad, slightly grey-green leaves clustered near the base of the stem. The flowers, up to five on a branching stem, are intense scarlet-orange with no central blotch and are up to 8cm in diameter when fully open. It is a native of Russian Tadjikistan and the Pamir-Alai mountains. In cultivation in Britain there is no need to lift the bulbs every year since it is easy to grow and flowers regularly.

T. saxatilis The plant which is generally grown under this name is a beautiful and easy tulip, increasing well by stolons but not always flowering very freely. The lowest leaf is up to 4cm broad and is very glossy green. The stem is 30–45cm in height and often branches in its upper half to produce two or three flowers, the upper one always larger than the lower. Each flower is about 6–8cm in diameter when fully open and of a bright pinkish-purple with a deep yellow centre. It occurs wild on Crete in rocky places. In Britain the usual flowering time is early May. The best patch of this I know is at Highdown in Sussex where it grows in shallow chalky soil on a hot dry slope facing the south coast. Undoubtedly it requires a thorough baking in the summer months.

T. sprengeri Being the last of all the tulips to flower, this is a very useful species. Indeed, as I write this, on 1st June, it is just about to open its first blooms. It usually grows about 35–45cm in height with rather narrow shiny green leaves. The flowers are 7–10cm in diameter, bright scarlet with a pale gold-buff exterior. It is said to have originated in Turkey, although it has not been rediscovered in recent years in the wild.

T. sprengeri is one of the easiest of all tulip species in Britain, seeding freely and reaching flowering size in only three years. It seems to do well in most situations and I have grown it in a south-facing border in full sun and currently have it at the foot of a peat garden facing north. Mrs Ruth McConnel has naturalized it in grass beneath poplar trees and I have seen it in masses in peat borders in the Shropshire garden of Mrs Netta Statham. In spite of this it remains very expensive in nurseries.

T. sylvestris One of the most widely distributed of tulip species, easily grown and an old favourite in British gardens. It grows up to 45cm in height but is usually about 30cm, with narrow, slightly grey-green stem-leaves. The flowers are pendent in bud but more or less erect when fully open, 6–8cm in diameter, yellow with a greenish-tinged exterior. It is a rare native of Britain but in Europe and Asia it extends from Portugal to Russia and Iran, usually growing in open woods, grassy or rocky places. In Turkey I have seen it forming huge colonies of up to an acre beneath pine trees. The form from Iran known as 'Tabriz' flowers more freely than the European plant. Subsp. *australis* from rocky Mediterranean areas is a smaller version with a pink-tinted exterior to the flower. *T. sylvestris* is suitable for planting in rock gardens and shrub borders or for naturalizing in grass or light woodland where it can be left undisturbed, for it does not need lifting for a summer rest period. It is not always free with its flowers.

T. turkestanica A rather dull species growing up to about 30cm in height with greyish leaves and a branched stem carrying five to nine smallish starry flowers which are white with a yellow centre, tinted with green externally. It is related to *T. biflora* and *T. polychroma* which are less robust versions of it, with fewer flowers. *T. turkestanica* grows wild in the Russian Tien-Shan and Pamir-Alai Mountains and is hardy in Britain. It will increase and flower well without lifting each year, given a sunny well-drained position, and is useful in that it flowers very early in February or March.

T. vvedenskyi Another of the huge scarlet tulips of central Asia which is sometimes obtainable. The height is about 35–45cm and the broad leaves are very greyish-green. Each brilliant red flower has a black centre, although some plants I have seen under this name have a yellow centre, and the spread is anything up to 20cm when it is open fully, far too large to be attractive, in my opinion. Being a plant of rocky places in southern-central Russia, it requires a hot dry summer and should be given a position in a warm border. The bulbs have the capability of pulling themselves down to a great depth in the soil and they continue to appear in my previous garden although the border was dug over when I left.

Urceolina Amaryllidaceae

A small genus of two species from the Andes of Peru and Bolivia. They are not quite hardy in England but make interesting pot plants for the cool greenhouse where they will flower in late spring before the leaves begin to lengthen. Propagation is very easy since the large daffodil-like bulbs produce many offsets which grow rapidly to flowering size. It is my experience that the bulbs flower better when pot-bound, as with quite a lot of the Amaryllidaceae. They can be kept fairly dry through winter whilst dormant.

U. peruviana (*U. miniata*) is the best-known species, with a small umbel of bright red or orange flowers on a stout stem up to 30cm in height. Each flower is carried on a long pedicel and is pendulous when fully open. The shape is that of an urn. The 2–4cm long tube is about 1cm wide in the middle, then constricted about two thirds of the way along and then widened again to the mouth. The stamens and style protrude considerably out of the flower. The leaves follow soon afterwards and are about 3–4cm wide, narrowed both at the base into a petiole and to an acute tip at the apex. Peru and Bolivia at 1900–3400m. *U. urceolata* (*U. pendula*) is less well known. It has wider (1·5cm) yellow flowers

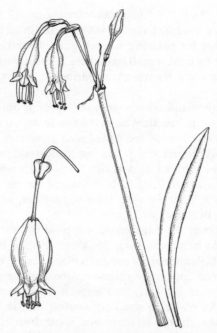

33 *Urceolina peruviana (and flower of U. pendula)*

about 6cm long, tipped with green. The leaves are large and elliptical, about 9–13cm wide, and usually present at flowering time. Peru.

Urginea Liliaceae

A rather uninteresting genus with a few Mediterranean species and a lot of dull African ones which are scarcely worth considering as garden plants, especially as they would need valuable greenhouse space here in Britain. *Urgineas* are bulbous with basal leaves and a racemose inflorescence of smallish starry flowers with six free segments, each with a brownish or greenish vein along the centre. Two northern hemisphere species are worth a mention but these are tender even in southern Britain and require either a cool greenhouse or a mild garden in the south-west.

U. maritima The Sea Squill. A very common plant around the Mediterranean, sometimes known as Crusaders' Spears. The inflorescence reaches·150cm and precedes the broad, glossy green leaves. The many whitish starry flowers are produced in a long dense raceme on very slender pedicels and are about 1–1·5cm in diameter. It grows in sandy or rocky places at low altitudes, the large bulbs often forming clumps near the surface. It flowers in autumn, the leaves following in winter and remaining green until the late spring. Although of no great garden value, the bulbs have been used for thousands of years for medicinal purposes, primarily in heart diseases.

U. undulata A shorter plant than *U. maritima*, at most 50cm in height, with a rosette of narrow, very undulate spreading leaves which appear after the flowers. The flowers are pinkish or greenish, about 2cm in diameter, produced in a fairly loose raceme. It is a much more local species than the preceding, occurring only in Sardinia, Corsica and North Africa east to Egypt in rocky places. The rosette of leaves is not unattractive but it is a tender plant for greenhouse or bulb-frame cultivation and therefore of doubtful value since there are many far more exciting plants which need the same space. Flowering in July to September in the wild.

Vallota Amaryllidaceae

There is one species only, *V. speciosa*, which is variously known as the Scarborough Lily, Berg Lily, George Lily or Knysna Lily. It is from South Africa and was discovered there in 1773 by Thunberg. The plant was introduced to Kew Gardens from this expedition by Masson who accompanied Thunberg, but it was soon to be a well-known plant in Europe. In about 1800, a Dutch ship carrying some bulbs to England was wrecked on the Yorkshire coast and the bulbs washed up. These were cultivated in nearby Scarborough and the common British name is the result, whereas the South African names describe the true home of *Vallota*. Its Latin name refers to Vallot, a French botanist who wrote a book about the garden of Louis XIII.

Vallota is not reliably hardy in Britain, although it will survive against a protected warm wall in the south. It is more usual to treat it as a pot plant in a cool greenhouse or windowsill, and although the bulbs seem to flower best when crowded into a pot, it is necessary to give regular liquid feeds in the spring growing season. In the wild *Vallota* is said to die down for a rest period, but in cultivation it is more or less evergreen. It should be given plenty of water in spring and summer and a partial rest in winter; that is, just enough moisture to keep the plant in leaf.

It is very closely related to *Cyrtanthus* but differs in its wide tapering perianth tube which is shorter than the segments. In *Cyrtanthus* the tube is normally much longer than the segments and roughly cylindrical. There are, however, a few species which do not fit into these generalizations, such as *C. guthrieae* and *C. sanguineus* and some botanists regard *Vallota* and *Cyrtanthus* as being one genus.

V. speciosa (*V. purpurea*) Grows to about 30cm in height when in flower and has six to 18 strap-like leaves per bulb, 1·5–3cm wide and up to 50cm in length, produced more or less in a fan. The flowers are produced in a small umbel, up to five per head and each one carried on a pedicel 2–3cm long. The six widely-spreading perianth segments are all equal, broadly obovate and joined into a funnel-shaped tube about 3–4cm long. When fully open the spread of the flower is about 6–9cm. The colour varies but the usual form is scarlet with a small white eye. A soft-pink form has been given the name var. *delicata*. In addition there is a red form with a large white eye, and a pure white form. Southern Cape, in the George, Uniondale, Knysna and Humansdorp areas in moist, cool, shady conditions. It flowers in Britain in August and September.

A hybrid between *Vallota* and *Cyrtanthus sanguineus* is in cultivation and is an attractive plant, more or less intermediate. It is less leafy than *Vallota*. Arends of Wuppertal made the cross between *Vallota* and *C. obliquus* but I can find no reference to this in cultivation now.

Veltheimia Liliaceae

Considering that there are only two species in this South African genus, there has been a surprising amount of confusion over the names. The correct names of the 'Winter Red Hot Pokers' have been sorted out by W. Marais in the *Journal of the Royal Horticultural Society* November 1972, page 483.

Veltheimias are bulbous plants, quite unrelated to *Kniphofia*, the true Red Hot Poker, which has fibrous or fleshy roots from a compact rhizome. Superficially there is some resemblance in the inflorescence, which is a dense spike of pendulous flowers, and the flowers are long and tubular. There the similarity ends, for *Veltheimias* produce basal rosettes of comparatively broad leaves, quite unlike the channelled, rather narrow ones of *Kniphofia* species. The fruits of *Veltheimia* are large (3–5cm long), with broad papery wings, and bear no relation to the much smaller, roundish or oblong, unwinged ones of *Kniphofia*. Both species make excellent pot plants for the temperate greenhouse, sun-lounge or windowsill. I find that annual re-potting is unnecessary but the plants are fed with a granular slow-release fertilizer in the autumn (e.g. 'National Growmore').

V. bracteata (*V. viridifolia*) This is the more robust species of the two with a cluster of bright shiny green basal leaves 6–8cm broad and a purplish-green spotted flower-stem up to 45cm in height. The long, tubular pendulous flowers are in a very dense but usually short raceme, each flower 3–4cm long and pinkish-red flecked with green and white. It inhabits coastal forest areas in the southern and eastern Cape from approximately Port Elizabeth east to Natal, at low altitudes. *V. bracteata* 'Rosalba' is a selection, having yellowish flowers tinted with red, especially towards the base of the tube. This is the easiest of the two species in cultivation and stays in growth through most of the year so does not require a dry dormant period. It flowers in winter, usually in January in England.

V. capensis (*V. glauca, V. roodeae*) This is a more delicate-looking plant than *V. bracteata* but in my experience is not quite as easy to grow and increase. The basal leaves are grey-green and narrower than those of *V. bracteata* and have distinctly undulate margins. The height is about the same but the inflorescence usually shorter and the flowers only 2–3cm long. These are pinkish-red in the form I grow but it appears to vary somewhat from wine-red to whitish spotted with red although I have not seen these forms. It flowers a little earlier than *V. bracteata* in my greenhouse, normally in December. South-west Cape, in rocky places and sometimes in shade, up to 1000m altitude. Unlike *V. bracteata* this goes completely dormant during the summer, requiring no water and a sunny spot at this time. *V. deasii* is a compact form of *V. capensis*, growing about 20cm in height with sturdy stems and short crisped-margined greyish leaves. The flowers are red and similar to those of *V. capensis*. It is not now considered to be a distinct species but is easily distinguishable by its habit and should perhaps be recognized as a variety or cultivar, since it makes a very attractive pot plant.

Watsonia Iridaceae

A wholly South African genus of *Gladiolus*-like plants with corms and a flat fan of rather stiff erect leaves. The inflorescence is a fairly dense raceme, sometimes branched, and the flowers are usually distichous, that is, alternate ones face in exactly opposite directions so that they are all in one plane. The flowers are rather tubular or narrowly funnel-shaped with a sharp bend in the lower third of the flower. The six perianth segments flare outwards somewhat.

There are several different types of *Watsonia* as far as cultivation in Britain is concerned, depending on their native habitat. Those from the eastern Cape are the most satisfactory since they are not in active growth during our winters, and these can be planted outdoors. Some of them originate from areas which do not have a prolonged dry period at any time and they are more or less evergreen. The south-west Cape species, the winter growers, are not hardy even in Surrey and I cannot report success with any of them, but at the same time I must admit to not having tried many of the species from this region. The few *Watsonias* I have tried have been planted in a warm sunny place, at the foot of a south-west fence. The best plants are growing in a frame which can be covered in winter and left uncovered in summer.

W. ardernei This grows to about 100cm when in flower, with a branched inflorescence carrying funnel-shaped flowers of pure white, with widely-flaring lobes. Although it is a south-west Cape species from Tulbagh it seems to behave as a summer grower here in Britain. Flowering June–August in southern England.

W. beatricis This is about 100cm in height with an unbranched spike of orange trumpet-shaped flowers flaring out at the mouth to about 5cm in diameter. Eastern Cape in damp areas, flowering June–August in Britain.

W. fourcadei A robust species up to 120cm in height with wide, very stiffly erect leaves. The branched flower-stem has closely-ranked narrowly tubular 6–7cm long flowers of a deep dull reddish-purple. This has been very satisfactory in my summer bulb-frame area, flowering in July. It occurs wild in the eastern Cape.

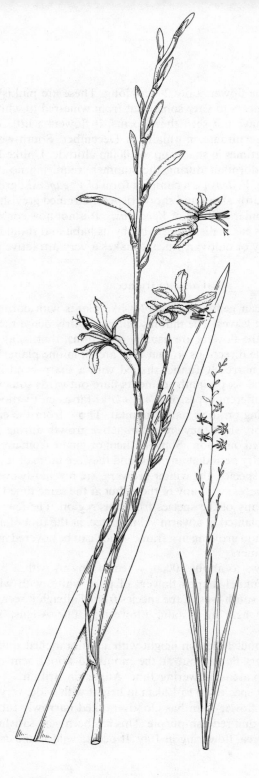

34 Watsonia angusta

W. wordsworthiana has been equally successful and is very similar but with flowers of an even deeper, more bluish shade of purple-red, while *W. angusta* is scarlet-red and has made large clumps in a bulb-frame.

W. versveldii Another robust species up to 150cm in height, which has a branched inflorescence with pink flowers having a red stain in the throat. This makes a lot of growth in the winter, being a south-west Cape species and needs some protection for this reason. It has however grown quite well in my bulb frame and flowers in late spring.

I have now obtained several species with a view to trying more of these beautiful plants, but as yet they have not flowered and I cannot comment upon their usefulness.

Zantedeschia Araceae

The Arum Lilies are African plants, occurring in damp or even marshy places from the Cape northwards to Angola, Malawi and Zambia. It is now generally considered that there are six species varying in the colour of the spathes from white to yellow, greenish or pinkish and sometimes with a purple blotch at the base. They are tuberous plants, producing tufts of large broad leaves which are sometimes beautifully mottled. The funnel-shaped spathes constitute the colourful part of the inflorescence, the minute petal-less flowers being carried on the spadix, a pencil-like organ which is enclosed by the spathe. Only one of the species is evergreen, *Z. aethiopica* and this too is the only one which is hardy in Britain. The rest are greenhouse plants which require a dry rest period when they die down.

Z. aethiopica This grows up to 60cm in height, with plain green broadly arrow-shaped leaves. The spathe is about 15cm in length, pure white shading to green towards the base, widely funnel-shaped, with the upper portion spreading out to one side and ending in a recurving tip. The spadix is bright yellow. It is a widespread plant in the wild from the south-west Cape east to Natal, Lesotho and Transvaal, and has a wide altitudinal range so that for British gardens the introduction of high-altitude plants would be worthwhile. It grows in marshy places. Although evergreen, *Z. aethiopica* can be grown as a waterside plant in southern England and mild western areas. The foliage becomes badly frosted in winter but new leaves are produced in spring. It is best planted with the tubers actually below water-level where they are protected from severe frost. The form known as 'Crowborough' is thought to be the hardiest available one in Britain. It will grow in sheltered borders near a warm wall and requires only a well-manured soil, flowering in early summer.

Zigadenus Liliaceae

A mainly North American genus of about 15 species, having a few Asiatic ones and one or two from Mexico and Guatemala. On the whole they are rather dull plants with smallish green flowers, but a few are rather striking and are easy to grow outdoors in Britain where they flower in summer. The species I have grown seem to enjoy ordinary well-drained soil in an open situation although they have succeeded in most places I have tried them, including raised peat beds.

Zigadenus are mainly bulbous plants with long linear basal leaves and much-reduced bract-like stem-leaves. The flowers are carried in a simple raceme or in a panicle and are usually flattish and white or green with glistening glands (nectaries) at the base of each segment.

Z. elegans This grows to about 70cm in height with 3–6cm wide greyish-green leaves. The flowers are usually borne in a raceme on 1–2cm long pedicels, and are 1·5–2cm in diameter. They are pale green, usually with a greyish 'bloom' on the segments. The nectary is yellowish-green and rather obvious in the form which I once grew. It is a very widespread species, growing in damp meadows, from Mexico north to Alaska. In the eastern parts of North America it is replaced by *Z. glaucus* which is regarded by S. J. Preece, who made a thorough study of the genus, as a variety of *Z. elegans*. There is little difference between the two and they apparently intergrade in their features. Flowering in mid to late summer and a useful plant for the peat garden, coming at a time when most of the plants have finished flowering.

Z. fremontii One of the best species I have grown, with a robust habit, reaching 70cm in height with leaves about half as long as the inflorescence and 1–3cm wide. The flowers are pale creamy greenish-yellow with a green nectary, about 1·5–2·5cm in diameter and produced in a raceme or, more rarely, a panicle. The nectary is notched at the apex making it botanically quite separate from *Z. elegans*, although from a horticultural viewpoint this seems a trivial matter. Southern Oregon and California in scrub on the coast ranges: Flowering early summer. This species prefers a well-drained situation, drying out somewhat in summer during the dormant period. Var. *minor* is a dwarf coastal form up to 15cm in height with fewer flowers.

Z. glaberrimus I have not cultivated this species but it appears to be one of the most striking and distinct of all the *Zigadenus*. It is robust, growing to about 100cm in height from a rhizome rather than a bulb and has tough linear leaves on the lower part of the stem, up to 2cm wide and rather stiffly erect. The inflorescence is a large, somewhat conical panicle, carrying many large creamy flowers, each 2–3cm in diameter. Each segment has a pair of nectaries at its base. It occurs in the south-east United States on coastal plains in marshy and sandy places. It seems likely that this would be a rather tender species in Britain, perhaps only suitable for southern and western parts, but since it is such an attractive species it would be worth trying.

Z. nuttallii 30–60cm in height with either a raceme or a panicle. The flowers are only 1–1·5cm in diameter, creamy-yellow with a rather poorly defined yellow nectary. It flowers in April or May. A plant of dryish grassy places in the central-southern states of North America. Although rather small-flowered, this makes up for lack of size by quantity, often producing very dense inflorescences.

Z. paniculatus Grows to about 50cm in height with leaves less than 2cm wide. The inflorescence is usually a panicle with small cream flowers less than 1cm in diameter. The nectary is greenish. Wild in dryish scrub areas of the western United States from Washington to New Mexico, flowering in May or June. As the perianth segments are small, the yellow stamens are very prominently displayed, a not unattractive feature of the species.

Z. venenosus This is rather similar to *Z. paniculatus* but has the three outer segments rather blunt at the apex compared with the very pointed ones of the latter species. The inflorescence is more often racemose than paniculate. It is very widespread in the western states of North America, from Canada south to Baja, California, flowering in April or May in grassy, often damp places.

GLOSSARY

Acid A soil which has a pH of less than 7, usually peaty; opposite of alkaline

Acuminate Long-pointed

Acute Pointed

Aggregate In botany, a group of closely related 'species' difficult to distinguish from each other

Alkaline Soil with a pH of more than 7; opposite of acid, often on chalk or limestone

Appendage An extra attachment to an organ, often of no apparent use

Axil The junction between leaf and stem

Axillary Growing from an axil

Basal Often applied to a leaf, meaning one arising from the base of the stem

Bifid Divided into two

Bract Modified leaf usually subtending the pedicel of a flower

Bulb Underground storage organ consisting of one to many fleshy scales attached to a basal plate of solid tissue, and enclosing a growing point

Bulbil Usually applied to small vegetative 'offsets' produced on the stem, or in the leaf axils, or in the inflorescence

Bulblet Small bulbs produced around the parent bulb

Calcareous Growing in chalky or limestone soils

Campanulate Bell-shaped

Capsule A dry seed pod which splits to shed its seeds

Chequered A regular mottling, usually rather geometrical, as in many fritillaries

Ciliate Fringed with hairs

Clone A plant propagated vegetatively so that all the individuals are genetically identical

Colony A group of individuals of a species

Concolorous Of a uniform colour

Cordate Heart-shaped

Corm Underground storage organ consisting of solid tissue, not scaly like a bulb

Corolla The collective name given to the whorl of petals of a flower

Corona An extra organ between the corolla and the stamens, as in the cup of a daffodil

Crest A ridge, usually yellow or orange coloured, on the 'falls' of an iris

Cultivar A form of a species or a hybrid which is considered distinct from the horticultural point of view, and nowadays given a non-latinized name

Cylindric Tube-like, with a circular cross-section

Dilated Swollen or expanded

Distichous Arranged in two rows; distichous rosette: flattened in one plane like the 'fan' of leaves of an iris

Endemic Confined to a given area, such as a mountain, island or country

Entire Usually applied to a leaf or perianth segment: undivided, with no teeth or lobes

Falcate Sickle-shaped

Fall Of an iris, the outer perianth segments which usually fall outwards and downwards

Filament The stalk of a stamen

Filiform Very narrow and thread-like

Fruit Any mature seed-bearing organ, whatever its form

Genus A natural group of plants all bearing the same generic name, e.g. *Narcissus*, subdivided into species having separate specific names, e.g. *Narcissus triandrus, Narcissus tazetta, Narcissus poeticus*

Glabrous Smooth, without any hairs

Gland In *Tigridia* and *Calochortus*, for example, an area on the perianth segments which secretes a sticky substance; the shape of the gland is often diagnostic

Glaucous Covered with a greyish waxy coat as with a cabbage leaf

Habitat The kind of locality in which a plant grows, e.g. wet grassy meadows, dry hillsides, scree slopes

Haft The narrow basal portion of the 'falls' or 'standards' of an iris flower

Hastate Spear-shaped, with the two basal lobes turned outwards

Herbarium A collection of dried specimens

Hybrid A cross between two different taxa of plants, either natural or artificial

Inflorescence Usually used to refer to the whole of the flower stem and flowers

Lanceolate Tapering at both ends but broadest just below the middle

Lax Loose, spaced out

Linear Narrow, the edges more or less parallel

Linear-lanceolate Very narrowly lanceolate, bordering on linear

Lobe Any projection of a leaf, perianth segment, etc.; sometimes used to refer to the segments themselves

Local Referring to distribution, a species which is not widespread

Monograph A written account of one particular group of plants, either a genus or family

Mouth Usually referring to the open end of a perianth tube

Naturalized Of foreign origin but reproducing and establishing as if a native

Nectary An organ in which nectar is secreted, usually at the base of a flower

Oblanceolate As in lanceolate, but broader just above the middle

Oblong Much longer than broad with nearly parallel sides

Obovate Reversed egg-shaped, the broadest end near the apex

Obtuse Blunt or rounded at the apex

Offset A small vegetatively produced bulblet at the base of a parent bulb

Opposite Usually of leaves, when two arise at the same node, one on each side of the stem

Orbicular Having a circular outline

Ovary The female portion of the flower containing the ovules, which after fertilization become the seeds; the ovary may be inferior, that is beneath the rest of the floral parts, or superior, inserted above the perianth

Ovate Egg-shaped

Palmate A leaf which has several lobes attached to the stalk like the fingers of a hand

Pedicel The stalk of a single flower

Peduncle Usually the main stalk of an inflorescence, each flower then being carried on a pedicel

Perianth The outer, usually showy part of a flower, in monocotyledons normally consisting of six segments, often in two whorls

Perianth tube The portion of the flower where the free segments become joined into a tube

Petiole The stalk of a leaf

Pinnate A compound leaf which has its leaflets arranged on either side of a common petiole

Pubescent Hairy

Raceme An inflorescence with the flowers carried on pedicels on an elongated peduncle, as in the bluebell

Rhizome A swollen rootstock capable of producing both roots and shoots, with dormant lateral buds and an apical shoot; may be above or below ground

Rosette A cluster of leaves densely packed together in circular form, usually flat on the ground, as in dandelion

Sagittate Arrow-shaped with the basal lobes enlarged into long 'barbs'

Scale One of the fleshy parts which go to make up a bulb

Sepal One of the segments which make up the calyx of a flower, the outer whorl of the perianth which often protects it in bud

Serrate Having teeth on the margin

Sessile With no pedicel, the flower carried directly on the peduncle

Spadix A spike of flowers on a thick fleshy axis, as in arums

Spathe A modified leaf, often much reduced and papery, enclosing the inflorescence in bud; may be one to several

Species The name given to the unit to which all the individuals of a particular kind of plant belong; in turn, the species belong to a genus

Spike The same as a raceme except that the flowers are sessile on the axis of the inflorescence, e.g. as in several *Muscari* species

Stamen The male part of the flower, consisting of anther and filament, and producing pollen

Staminode A sterile stamen, often modified and enlarged

Standard The inner perianth segments of an iris flower, which in many species are erect

Sterile A flower which is incapable of producing seeds because of some deformity

Stigma The tip of the female part of the flower, which receives the pollen

Stolon An underground stem produced by a bulb which gives rise to further young bulbs

Style The portion of the female part of a flower between the ovary and the stigma

Subspecies A group of individuals within a species, not differing sufficiently from other groups to be given a higher (i.e. species) classification

Synonym A superseded or unused name

Taxonomy Classification

Tendril An extension, usually of a leaf, which is capable of twining around other objects for support

Terra-rossa Red earth, clay-like and common in Mediterranean regions; the habitat of many bulbs

Tessellated Chequered, as in many *Colchicum* and *Fritillaria* species

Throat The upper part of a perianth tube

Toothed A margin which is jagged with teeth-like projections

Trifid Three-lobed

Trumpet In *Narcissus* species, often used to denote the corona when it is longer than cup-shaped

Tuber A swollen subterranean organ, often capable of producing shoots from dormant buds

Tunic The coat of a bulb

Umbel An inflorescence like the spokes of an umbrella, as in most *Allium* species

Variety A division of plants subordinate to a species and subspecies

Whorl The arrangement of parts of a plant in a circle around an axis, as in the leaves of the Crown Imperial (*Fritillaria imperialis*) and some lilies

Widespread Distributed over a wide area, but not necessarily common in any one place

Index